ELIZABETH SHASSERE

BECOMING A
FEARLESS
LEADER

A simple guide to taking control
and building happy, productive,
highly performing teams

Visit my website at www.elizabethshassere.com

ISBN: 978-1-9999932-0-7

Table of Contents

Chapter 5: Why culture matters to your team when it comes to getting things done 79

Chapter 6: Knowledge and Information: How getting the balance just right gives you a competitive edge.. 89

Chapter 7: Why your team's physical environment is the most important thing you'll never notice ..107

What not to do (based on my own mistakes)...... 122

Chapter 8: How to put it all together and finish strong- The Workbook 125

Introduction: How I became a fearless leader (after being fired by sticky note)

"…in every organization everyone rises to the level at which they become paralyzed with fear." -Seth Godin, Tribes (2008)

"Elizabeth, you have been terminated from this job…"

My stomach fell into my shoes as I plucked the sticky note from my computer monitor and read that first line. I pulled out my chair, sat down with a thump, and forced myself to read on.

"…and have been moved into the director's position at [….]".

Wait. What?

Was I being fired or promoted? And who does either of these things by sticky note? In such a publicly visible place?

Where my stomach had fallen, panic was starting to rise. I didn't know how to be a director! I wasn't ready!

In that moment I seriously considered a total freak-out. I would run screaming to my boss, or chain myself to my desk and refuse to move to the new job.

In the next moment I got angry. Who treats their employees this way? Who thinks it's ok to do something like this by sticky note?

That thought turned my anger to pure determination. I decided right then and there that I would pick up their sticky gauntlet and run with it.

I had come to learn many of the faults and foibles of the public sector organisation I worked in. The limitations of its human resources department was legendary. But this took the biscuit.

I would show them.

I also vowed that in my new position as a leader, I would never be so wretched in my duties that I would communicate decisions by sticky note.

So began my unexpected catapult from wet-behind-the-ears assistant director to executive director of my own department.

I'd been doing the technical work in my area of expertise for about ten years. Now, as an executive director, I was going to be in charge of all the legal responsibilities for my own department. This promotion would also make me a board member, giving me statutory responsibilities for things like governance, financial accountability, and due diligence. To say it was an intimidating prospect is an understatement.

I had to figure out how to get a grip on this knee-weakening new responsibility.

******

I was lucky that I was probably in a better position than most people who are thrown into the deep end of management. I had at least completed various management programmes as part of my professional training and registration as a public health consultant. You know the type: canned workshops that take you through the motions, make you do personality assessments and role plays, that sort of thing. But no amount of theoretical training can truly prepare you for doing these things for the first time in real life.

This is not to say that those programmes don't have value. I have personally gained a lot from understanding my own working styles and preferred methods based on my innate strengths and weaknesses. But workshops in which you are more concerned with if they will have the good biscuits or if you will get out in time to beat the traffic is not the same as the experience of managing and leading real people in real, unpredictable situations.

I'd been in my previous role as an assistant director role for less than two years in a small, underfunded department. I was hired to support the director who had been a bit of a one-man band for too long. I didn't even have my own team to manage. We all felt more like pioneer survivalists than a department responsible for statutory duties to protect the public's health. I felt like I still had a lot to learn and a lot to do before becoming the head honcho.

In all, I worked for 20 years in public health for government agencies. I first managed programmes, then programmes and a few people. Then, suddenly, thanks to my sticky note promotion, I was managing a lot of people while they dealt with the programmes and day to day business.

Many people cite the stability of government jobs as one of their perks (30 years followed by a nice pension), but the public sector is certainly not without its drawbacks and limitations.

For me, the worst qualities are the unwieldiness of the bureaucracy, the aversion to change, innovation, and risk, and territoriality between departments and agencies.

The senior management and leadership structures are rife with people who are just waiting out their time, looking forward to their retirement, and wanting an easy life in the meantime. They have usually been around for decades, they don't like change, and new ideas make them twitchy.

If you're a newcomer and attempt to shake things up a bit, you could be in for a rough ride. I was that newcomer, and at times the ride was very rough. The phrase *"But we've always done it this way"* would spur me to action. I wanted to introduce some innovation and modernisation. When done for the right reasons, it is worth the effort and aggravation.

I worked hard for those 20 years trying to change and improve things. In fact, I worked too hard and too many hours for too long (to the detriment of almost all other aspects of my life).

The resource restrictions in the public sector tested me to my limits. Funding is always tight, and I had to get good very quickly at being able to accomplish my legally-mandated work with little or no money. I had to learn the art of begging, influencing, and persuading partner organisations to collaborate to get work done.

I was always short-staffed and short of the skill sets I needed. I ended up working long hours trying to do everything myself, or trying to come up with ways to influence the organisation so it would recognise the value of our department's work and properly support it. When I couldn't get the job done, I would be stressed out and exhausted with the frustration of it all. I no longer felt like I was making progress. I felt like I was in a never-ending battle with my own organisation, and the battle was futile.

The innate institutional faults meant that the internal functions of the organisation suffered. Systems and processes were often in shambles. Departments and teams were running on luck and good will. Staff were struggling every day just to get the basics done.

Each time I took over a new department, it was in a worse state than the last one, and I learned a lot of hard lessons. I went through some terrifying situations and made a lot of mistakes. Over time, I devised a systematic and manageable approach to tackling even the most dysfunctional team and turning it around quickly.

This is what I want to share with you here. What follows is simple-to-follow guidance and easy-to-use templates that will help you become a fearless and effective leader.

Who this book is for

"...fearlessness is not the absence of fear, it's the mastery of fear. Fearlessness is about getting up one more time than we fall down — or are tripped by our critics!" - *Ariana Huffington*

I pulled together the lessons I learned and the tools I developed so that you don't have to struggle like I did. I want this guide to help you skip the scariest and most difficult bits of being a manager, especially when faced with a tough, challenging situation. It is a smart, constructive, yet simple way to get a grip and get rid of any fear so you can be a great leader as quickly as possible.

Whether you are brand new in your first job or a seasoned professional who wants to turn around a problematic team, or simply make some improvements, this guide will get you there.

This book is for you if:

- You are considering taking on a role with management responsibilities for the first time.
- You have been at it for years but are struggling to get the outcomes you want.

- You think your team needs a tune-up to improve performance, outputs, or morale, or even to improve recruitment and retention.

It will take the fear out of situations and give you a sense of control if:

- You often feel like a fraud and worry that people will discover that you are out of your depth or aren't capable of the job. (Imposter Syndrome)
- You have been quickly promoted up to a manager's position because you were good at your profession, but haven't had much education or training in managing teams. (The Peter Principle)

I've been in all these situations. That fear of the unknown, or that horrible pang of anxiety in the centre of your chest, can take you from confident and capable professional to floundering manager in a heartbeat.

These feelings alone create a crisis of confidence that can make you forget that you actually do have skill sets and experience to draw on. When I faced my most complex, difficult situations, it was always made worse when I questioned my ability to make a decision or solve the problem. When I had no confidence in my ability or my ideas, I became immobilised and did nothing. It's like when you stop treading water- that's when you start to sink.

The tools in this guide are what helped me stop that downward slide every single time.

Of course, things may not be this bad for you. I hope that you are working in a much more supportive environment than I was and that you're not fighting a daily battle. It was not always this bad for me. I did have some positive experiences and worked with some excellent bosses. Even in the best situations, change can be good and offer new opportunities for you and your team.

When one organisation I was working in got a new chief, I felt a whole new opportunity arise. All the baggage of the old guard was gone. I could try and persuade a new leader that the work of my team was good, important, and worthy of organisational support. I wanted our work to be valued, and I wanted to be seen to be a manager who could get things done, use corporate resources constructively, and get a good return on investment. I used the methods in this guide to improve our performance as a team and get noticed.

When I took on new teams, I wanted my new staff to feel comfortable and confident in me as early as possible. I wanted them to know that I was there to take stock and create a supportive and effective department that made everyone's quality of work life just that bit better.

That's why this guide can also help you if:

- You have a new boss who is getting the measure of her new staff (you may want to impress them, or at least get their attention).
- You have a new team who is getting the measure of you (as their new boss).
- You want to show a real impact fast: you want to ask for a raise, go for a promotion, or improve future prospects.

It's also a useful guide for mapping out those infamous first 100 days in a new job to make sure you start as you mean to go on- from a position of confidence and strength.

How this book can help you become a fearless leader

I am a big believer in working smarter, not harder. I learned the lessons in this guide the hard way, and these tools were developed through trial and error. I am confident that they will make your job easier, and that they will make you a better manager and leader.

The tools here will help you quickly and easily take control of the most important things that make up the foundation of your responsibilities as a leader and a manager, including:

- Building a united team that works together effectively, and is loyal to you as the leader as well as to each other
- Conducting effective and powerful one-to-ones and annual performance reviews that get the

most out your staff, and help you build a strong and mutually respectful relationship with one another

- Using a simple four-part model to analyse, troubleshoot, and improve the overall quality of your team

There were many times in my career when I thought I could no longer face the challenges that were being thrown my way. I had bosses that wanted me to fail. I had bosses that put no value on my profession. I experienced major political upheavals that undermined the status of the legal basis for my programmes. I fought against people who thought I was too young to be a leader, or didn't like the fact that I was one of very few women in my role.

All of these things added to a job that already came with monumental complexities and responsibilities. The tools in this guide helped me not only to survive, but to thrive in that role and build some of the strongest personal relationships in my life.

Four years ago I left that career to go into business for myself. I am now an entrepreneur with a company that uses accessible tech for public consultation and feedback. These tools and the lessons I learned during 20 years in the public sector continue to serve me well, even in such a vastly differently environment.

That's why I'm sure that no matter what situation you find yourself in, if you are managing and leading a small team or a large one, in any industry, the practical tools in this guide can help.

I want to share them with you.

All of the tools can also be found online in full-size pdf versions on my website at www.elizabethshassere.com.

Elizabeth Shassere

Chapter 1: How to build a united team that works together

*In winning companies, everybody pulls in
the same direction. -Steve Blank*

In my first job that involved managing others, I was responsible for just one person. One.

She was twice my age and had decades more experience working in the health system than I did. She could have made my first experience miserable enough to put me off managing for life. She could have been dismissive and disrespectful to me because of my youth and inexperience. I could have been powerless to actually manage her at all.

But using the tools I am going to tell you about in this chapter, the situation was a success. There may only have been the two of us, but by developing a strong and constructive relationship, we became a team. We developed mutual respect for each other. We still keep in touch to this day, although she is long retired.

The quality and performance of your team will make or break you as a leader. It will make your daily working life a living hell or a make it the reason you look forward to going into the office every day.

I will use the word 'team' throughout this guide. In this context, it means anything from me and my one staff member (or you and your team of three mailroom staff), all the way through to a team of executive directors and you as their chief executive.

Team: /tiːm/ : noun : 1) two or more people working together; 2) a group of players forming one side in a competitive game or sport

This guide will help anyone who has responsibility for managing any group of people responsible for a certain function. You may be a **team leader**, a **department manager** or **head**, or the **CEO** of a company.

Regardless, the tools and methods I share in this guide will help you and the people you are responsible for work better together. It will support the development of your relationship with your teammates and establish you as their leader.

Susan, that first person I managed, had a lot of confidence in her own ability. In turn, she was magnanimous about the fact that I was having my first chance to manage. She wanted me to have a good learning experience. She respected my technical education and training, and I was able to provide her with useful guidance about the programmes she was leading.

I was also fortunate to have an excellent manager myself, from whom I learned some powerful management techniques when it came to offering supervision and guidance to team members.

It would be a few years before the sticky note incident that would propel me into executive-level responsibilities, but the simple methods I honed during this experience with Susan gave me the basic skills I needed on day one when I walked into my new department.

******

When the day of the sticky note incident came, I had no time at all to prepare for my new job as a director. It turns out my boss's boss had been pulled up by the regulators for having a vacancy in a statutory department, and he needed me in there ASAP.

I became a victim of the Peter Principle.

The Peter Principle says that when you are good at your profession, (or in my case, when your boss is desperate!), you may keep getting promoted until you are operating beyond your level of competency. You will do less of what you are good at, that got you noticed in the first place, and more managing people and leading teams.

Instead of succumbing to the rules of the Peter Principle, I was determined to make a good job of the situation. I refused to cave in under the pressure. But in truth, my emotions were swinging almost hourly between bolshy bravado ("I'm gonna be the best manager they've ever had") to abject terror ("they aren't going to listen to a word I say, they're going to hate me, and I will fail miserably and end up in a disciplinary procedure for not fulfilling my responsibilities").

I was feeling sorry for myself, but then it dawned on me that my new sticky note team had become victims, too. It's a matter of pure luck whether the promoted person becomes the best leader you ever had or if they become a brusque, hard-nosed tyrant who is trying to cover up the fact that they have no idea what they are doing.

One of the biggest saboteurs of confidence and performance in a job is the feeling of being a fraud, of being found out to be unable to do what you were hired to do. Imposter Syndrome is a powerful double edge sword- you can think of yourself as a fraud and you can also believe that everyone else thinks so too. Your self-belief dwindles to nothing and it can become a self-fulfilling prophecy as you get too scared to take action and make necessary decisions.

I knew that having a framework and tools was essential for me to hold my nerve and not lose the last crumb of faith I had in myself. I had to believe I could do the job, and that I could get everyone on side.

I knew I needed something to hang onto in order to feel confident in myself. But more importantly, I needed my new team to have at least a kernel of confidence in me so that I didn't crash and burn in that first week.

I dug deep into my toolkit of experience, limited as it was, and I thought about what I considered was the most important thing I could do as a new leader in this situation. The answer I found was a cure-all solution to my problems.

The leadership cure-all for Imposter Syndrome and the Peter Principle

Stay humble.

Humility is the most important characteristic of an effective leader. It can get you out of tight spots. It can turn around negative situations, including those that seem doomed to ruin team relationships as well as performance.

This is what humility as a leader looks like in practice:

- Get comfortable saying "I don't know", or "I need help".
- Ask a lot of questions. Do a lot of listening.
- Ask others to step up and let them shine.
- Don't be afraid to make mistakes. Admit to them quickly, apologise when you get it wrong, and ask for help to make it right.
- Ask how you can make the situation better for others.
- Stretch your team and invest in their development.

I realise this may not be as easy as it sounds. When we find ourselves feeling threatened, anxious, or like there is too much at stake, one of our first instincts as humans is to get defensive and hostile. My natural instinct when I find myself under pressure is to come out swinging- I'm a fighter not a flighter- and I've had to learn to stop, breathe, and think constructively about how to salvage a volatile situation.

There can be a tendency to tear down others in order to feel less threatened by them, or to bluster over our insecurity and bully our way into convincing people that we are capable of the job. *This method almost always backfires.* You will be quickly found out. You will be alienated from your team and become a less effective leader.

It's a miserable feeling when you lose your team. It's like being a football manager who has "lost the dressing room". You treat your team badly, or fail them one too many times, and one day you'll walk into that room full of sweaty, weary players and immediately tell by body language and facial expressions that you no longer have their respect. And they certainly don't like you any more. You can be sure they aren't going to take your direction. Any chance of regaining that winning streak dwindles to nothing.

Humility can help you avoid getting into that position, or at least help you turn it around if you find yourself there.

In my very first management experience with my-one-team-member-Susan, I didn't bluster through my one-to-ones with her acting as though I knew more than her about the health system we were working in. I was willing to ask her how I could add value by offering to share my knowledge and expertise without pretending to be something I wasn't. *I asked how I could make the situation better for her.*

And she showed humility when she accepted my technical and subject matter guidance and listened to my views on how to run her programme. *She asked me a lot of questions, and listened carefully to my responses.*

My boss at the time needed help to take some of the pressure off of her from having too many staff to manage. She took a punt on me. *She let me step up and shine.*

This is the foundation of the talent that marks an effective leader: **learning to work with and through others**. This requires humility.

I was committed to open and honest communication. I went on to build a highly-performing team made up of people who liked and respected each other. Little did I know then just how valuable that experience was going to be in one of my next jobs, when I was faced with one of the worst experiences of my working life.

A strong and united team is your secret weapon

It wasn't a meeting; it was an interrogation.

I walked back to my office in a daze and immediately rang the woman who had been my mentor for the past several months. For what felt like an age, I couldn't even speak beyond just letting her know who was on the other end of the phone. She could tell instantly that something was wrong.

When I finally felt like I could talk, I couldn't decide whether to burst into tears or burst out laughing. I ended up doing a bit of both. I took a deep breath and started at the beginning.

I had gone to the chief executive's office for what was supposed to be a routine one-to-one meeting. When I walked in, the finance director was also there. Usually, there was a small coffee table with a clover of four chairs around it, but they had taken one of the chairs away so there were only three. They had moved two together on one side and put the third directly across from them. The chief exec and finance director sat together and motioned for me to sit in the facing chair- all that was missing was the bare lightbulb shining in my face.

It didn't take a detective to realise something was up, and that this wasn't going to be the usual state-of-the-finances catch-up.

My first reaction was amusement. They looked like two little boys wanted to recreate a scene from a spy movie they had seen and were relishing playing at "making the enemy talk". The amusement didn't last long, as I also realised they must be up to no good to go to all this trouble to try and intimidate me.

Many years had passed since the sticky note incident and my first day with that brand new department. I had a lot more confidence in myself. I had seen the best and worst of the health service and local government, and I had been thinking of a career change for a few years. I was not prepared to take any crap.

I sat down. I was poised, professional, and all smiles. They told me they were commandeering my department's budget and that I had to tell everyone it was my idea and that I was glad to hand it over. That was the gist of it, anyway.

I couldn't decide if I was more outraged by the fact that they were trying this strong-arm method, or that they truly thought I would agree to it. I refused their demand. Let me tell you how I got out of that one and why I was able to do it.

There was a lot going on in the organisation due to national policy changes and new laws. Most importantly, the way we were funded was about to change. In many organisations just like mine, the big bosses were choosing to interpret this as an opportunity to take resources away from our department and redirect it to some politically sensitive areas that were facing budget pressures.

All over the country, directors like me were fighting to keep our programmes funded. The integrity, or lack thereof, of our chief execs and the politicians in our local authorities were determining just how big of a fight each of us had on our hands.

The strength of our teams was determining whether we won the battles (or the size of our defeats). I had a strong team, but the fight was dirty.

A strong and united team is your secret weapon. A strong team is earned. It is built, cultivated, and cared for.

The strength of a team has two facets. Firstly, it is determined by how loyal you are to each other, how well you support each other, and how well you treat each other behind closed doors. Secondly, it is determined by how you present yourselves as a team to the outside world.

Let me explain:

In this organisation, our team, and certainly me as its leader, felt targeted and undermined. Locally, budgets were in crisis. Programmes were failing. Our budget was seen as a soft target, even though it was supposed to be protected by law.

Directors like me were given sole responsibility for our funding, rather than it being in the domain of the chief executives. This was expressly so those budgets would be protected from the pilfering that I was experiencing in my chief exec's office that day. He thought he could get around it by coercing me to say I was giving it over wilfully.

This was his last ditch effort. All his other attempts had failed to make a chink in my team's armour. He had been instructing the finance department and other competing functions to find a way to take our money.

We were put through intense interrogations about our spending. We were forced to sit through whole days of panels to try and prove that we had committed funding that was unnecessary. The finance director created a hostile and bullying atmosphere. It was a waste of everyone's time and energy, as we had evidence behind every penny we had committed. And the fact was, there couldn't be a change to the spending without my sign off.

When the panels didn't work, individual team members were isolated and asked to betray the work of the department. Essentially, they were asked to act as traitors and admit that the evidence was wrong or contrived, or that the programmes were poorly performing and that our budget was being spent wastefully.

But I had worked hard to build a united team, one that realised the value of presenting a united front. This meant that we were all always on message. We spoke with one voice. We stood up for each other, especially when one of us wasn't there to defend ourselves. We conducted ourselves with loyalty and integrity even when faced with the intense pressure of politicians or executives who had the future of our department in their hands.

It wasn't easy. It was a constant battle and it took its toll on all of us. At first, our strong common voice rattled the establishment. This only made the pressure on us worse. It shocked the old guard who were used to getting their way and having their bidding done. They hadn't seen anything like it.

But we not only felt passionate about our jobs, we were also legally bound to do what was right for the public based on evidence. I was responsible, by law, for making sure our funding was spent on the right things, for the right reasons.

This would not have been possible if I had been dealing with a disunited or fractious team. If we had not stood together, not only would I not have been able to do my job properly, I would have cracked under the pressure. I would have felt betrayed and isolated. The fight wouldn't have been worth it, and I would have had very little chance of holding my position. But I had created a team that could withstand the pressure, and in the next section I will explain how I did that.

You can create a team fit for a fearless leader

While humility is the personal quality that helped make my first management experience a good one and set me up for taking on that first big team, humility alone won't get the job done.

Humility on its own will just make you a doormat. It sends a signal to your team that you rely on them 100% to get anything done and have no ideas or abilities of your own. Used wrongly, it makes you look weak and ineffective.

Being humble makes it possible for you to build a great team because humility allows you to *act with integrity and to foster loyalty*.

Humility, integrity, and loyalty are the starting ingredients you need to create a united team that will get things done and weather those inevitable rough patches.

As the leader, you need to make it clear what the expectations are in your team and you should lead by example:

- You speak well of each other.
- You stick up for each other when dealing with external partners.
- You demonstrate that your team is all on the same side by knowing the key messages and sticking to them, even when challenged.

You may not realise just how much people pay attention to all that you do when you are the leader. Team members note how leaders respond in certain situations, and they pick up, even when they don't realise it, what your values are and what you consider to be favourable or important.

A leader builds on this each day, in face-to-face time with individuals, in team meetings, during discussions, when working on projects. You must model behaviour that is important to you, such as treating others with respect, being honest, and valuing each person's contribution. These will then become the norm within your team.

I know from my own experience that this isn't as easy as it sounds.

A team so strong it can defeat the enemy within it

I once had a team member who turned out to be the biggest hiring mistake of my career. I hope to never meet anyone as toxic and divisive as Paula again. She would pick fights, lie about what other people did (or didn't do), and constantly criticise every one of her teammates. As soon as I realised my mistake, I started the process to get rid of her. In the public sector, this was a bureaucratic nightmare and took many months.

This was especially frustrating because of how I'd built up the camaraderie in my team. I knew that just like in a family, creating a respectful and supportive atmosphere in a team is not all warm hugs and good manners. We needed some ground rules.

My rules were simple, really. We agreed that team meetings, or any time we were behind closed doors, was a safe space to argue and air differences. We could fight and disagree, criticise each other (respectfully), and otherwise hash it out. But as soon as the door opened, or we were in the company of our colleagues or external partners, we were all on message again.

I could think my teammate was the dimmest, laziest miscreant on the planet, or be so angry I could tear him to pieces. But as soon as I was speaking to someone outside our team, I spoke about him with respect or I said nothing at all.

I can only imagine how the situation with the pilfered budget and the intimidation attempt would have gone if we, as teammates, had been caught out. If any one of my staff had said to the finance director, "*Yeah, that Elizabeth, she means well and tries hard, but she really doesn't have a clue. I can't believe she put so much of the budget into the heart disease prevention programme*", or, "*Well, maybe you can't*" *fault her professionalism, but she is the drippiest leader you'll ever come across, and that accent of hers- it really grates!!".*

Even the slightest chink would have presented a weakness that could have been exploited and undermined our work entirely. But because my staff had plenty of opportunity to challenge me in private about my budget or programme decisions, which I encouraged, there was little room for dissent outside of the department.

These types of interactions have to be carefully managed, but allowing them to take place in a protected environment means that grievances don't spill out into external work. This way, we don't appear as a group of fractious individuals infighting and back-biting; it's essential for survival when someone is trying to divide and conquer us as a team.

Conducting ourselves in this way also helped us develop our relationship. We became committed to supporting one another. It quickly broke down the defences and barriers that can exist when you are just getting to know your teammates. This is how I took on my first new department after the sticky note incident. I consider establishing these values as one of the most urgent and important actions I take with new teams:

- **I make it clear that dissent is acceptable and welcome as long as it is in the privacy of the team meeting or one-to-one.** If anyone has a problem with me, a teammate, a decision, or action taken, it is fair to bring it up constructively (preferably with an alternative or a solution), but privately.

- **I coach my team to learn to take constructive criticism, by me as well as by their teammates, on the chin.** I do this by ensuring anyone with a criticism brings a suggestion of how to do it better, or a new solution, or an offer of help to get a job done. This means that we all get a chance to use the situation to improve and grow. We come to realise that offering and receiving constructive criticism and advice is a valuable part of being in a loyal and protective team.

- **We all agree that we speak highly of each other to external partners.** Reputations are made and broken by offhand, incidental remarks about colleagues and managers. It is an extremely powerful tactic for becoming an effective and successful part of your company to help foster good reputations for each other outside of the team bubble. It is a point of integrity.

- **I make an unbreakable rule that outside of a private team environment, your loyalty is unquestionable.** Exchanges can get heated, or slagging matches may kick off, but the minute you walk out of that room, you never tell tales or break confidences. If any one of our team members does this, they give our power away as a team and make it harder on everyone to get stuff done.

- **Because I stress the importance of integrity, everyone knows that there is no room for blind loyalty.** I draw the line at lying, spreading rumours, or painting unrealistic pictures of capabilities or accomplishments just to 'big up' the team or protect wrongdoing. There is never an excuse for covering up corruption or breaches in safety. But because of the internal processes we have in place, it is highly unlikely we would get to this point. Teammates feel able to call out bad behaviour long before there is a need to whistleblow.

Leading and managing teams is not easy, and certain circumstances can make it a lot harder. No matter why you may be struggling as a leader, whether or not you get your team on board will make or break you.

A leader with a united team is perceived as capable and effective. This can grease the wheels for better collaboration, getting required information or approvals, and it will certainly make a more positive working environment. It can also help you weather any challenges you may face, such as changes in organisational leadership or threats to the sustainability of the company.

In summary:

- Creating a united team is essential to your success as a leader and a manager.
- Humility in leadership is necessary for creating this team.
- Humility, integrity, and loyalty together make it possible to build a strong and united team.

- The way your team presents themselves to external partners, both as a team and as individuals, determines the reputation and effectiveness of it.

In the next chapter

You may be thinking that creating a united team that is loyal and acts with integrity is easier said than done. A team is made up of individuals and to get every single one of them to always act in the best interests of the team is a tall order. But I have a tried and true method for bringing individuals on board and making it more likely that you will develop the team you want.

One of the fastest and most effective ways to build a united team is through a strong and constructive performance review process. In the next chapter, I will take you through how I conduct one-to-one meetings with my team members. I will share with you the simple form that has worked for me for years, and has been adopted by many of my colleagues.

Chapter 2: Why one-to-ones and performance reviews are your most powerful tools

"Just being available and attentive is a great way to use listening as a management tool. Some employees will come in, talk for twenty minutes, and leave having solved their problems entirely by themselves." - Nicholas V. Luppa

As stoic and resilient as I believed myself to be, even I couldn't deny that the stress of my situation was beginning to take its toll on me physically. I was going to have to ramp up my efforts to get rid of Paula, or I would be the one out the door on sick leave.

Yes, this is "the-biggest-hiring-mistake-of-my-career" Paula. She was terrorising my department and all my team members. I was consulting HR, my fellow directors, and my mentor for help. They gave their best advice, but because we were working in a government agency there were strict processes to follow.

Luckily, the first rule in these strict processes was one I had always made part of my management practice: document, document, document. Even if it was a short, bulleted phrase in a paper diary, if anything unusual or just not quite right occurred, I would jot down a little reminder to myself in my notes. This practice has saved my bacon on many occasions.

Every time Paula pulled one of her stunts, or made comments that were just 'off', or did one of a million of the truly disturbing things that disrupted the team, I would make a note.

I dreaded our one-to-one meetings. I had even started to leave the door open during them. But I stuck to the form, and treated her just like every other team member in those situations. And I wrote everything down.

For months, I couldn't do much more than offer a listening ear to my staff when they needed to vent about being the brunt of one of Paula's latest terrors.

I also referred them to our organisation's employee assistance programme, and agreed for them to have any time they needed away from the office to take up those services. I encouraged and supported them in doing their own documentation exercises. Not only did it help them work through what was happening, it provided additional evidence that proved the effects of Paula's behaviour. This additional documentation showed that it was not just one person's perspective, or even misperception, that her conduct was destructive and unacceptable.

I was also able to progress things more quickly by making the case that my number one concern was protecting my staff from this person. Their written experiences gave us the proof that she was something we all needed protecting from.

Then, one day, when Paula's reign of terror reached fever pitch, I was able to have her escorted from the premises with the documentation to back up my decision. Good riddance!

Although it can be regarded as a triumph for my one-to-one documentation system, it is also a failure for me as a manager that I ever hired her in the first place. It is one of my biggest regrets that I couldn't manage her behaviour and protect her teammates from her.

Without that documentation, I could have found myself in a tribunal or even a lawsuit, while the rest of my team dealt with the daily chaos.

This is an extreme story that I hope no one ever has to deal with. With the other 99% of my staff, these one-to-ones and the documentation that went with them were simply valuable performance management tools that meant that we could record great work, commit to support for improvements, and strengthen our relationships through active listening.

******

You will find templates for one-to-ones, and all the materials mentioned, in the workbook at the back of this book. You can also get full-size pdf versions from my website at www.elizabethshassere.com.

******

One-to-ones: you can't build a strong team without them

One-to-ones have many different names in the workplace. They are simply the time you take to sit down face-to-face with someone that you manage and talk about their work, their performance, and generally just about how they are getting on in their role.

During one-to-ones you might discuss needing more time to complete something, or wanting to get additional training. Someone might need help with a difficult workplace relationship. They may need some advice on how to handle an awkward co-worker.

One-to-ones: /wun too wuns/: When a manager actively listens to an individual, that individual believes they have been heard, and both agree action that will be taken on both sides.

I use a template with these headings:

- Informal discussion
- Current workload and priorities update (to be completed by the team member prior to the meeting)
- Update on progress against objectives (to be completed by the team member prior to the meeting)
- Key issues/action forward (for the manager to complete based on the discussion and shared with team member)

Informal discussion- Starting with a few minutes of general catch up is a good way to get to know new team members, or let them get to know you if you are new. It helps set the tone of the meeting so it doesn't feel like an inquisition, 'test', or like being in the headmaster's office ready to be told off. You can also get a good idea of how that person is getting on in the workplace. Are they happy in their role? Do they enjoy working there? Are they under a lot of stress? Do they seem disengaged or uncommitted to the work? It's meant to be a two-way conversation, but with all one-to-ones, you should be doing the vast majority of the listening.

Current workload and priorities update- After the initial discussion, it's your team member's chance to take you through their main pieces of work and the tasks that are taking up most of their time. This is a good time to make sure that you agree that they are focusing on the things that are most important to the company. Some people get caught up in pet projects, spend too much time on the things they enjoy the most, or on the things they find easiest, at the expense of company priorities.

You will also get an idea of whether their workload is too heavy or too light. They may have too much on, or be under too much stress to do a good job, or they could have the capacity to pick up some slack from other members of the team.

Update on progress against objectives- Once you've gone over the current workload and priorities, you should have a good overview of whether the work that is being done is supporting agreed annual objectives.

This is a good exercise for keeping things like 'drift' in check. Drift is when workloads veer away from agreed priorities because of external demands or individuals' interest in certain topics. Done regularly, this can easily help your team get back on track and realise when they are missing the mark.

This part of the discussion is also what sets you up for a smooth and efficient annual performance review. In the next section, I will describe objective-setting and performance reviews, and show you why doing one-to-ones this way makes reviews so much easier and effective.

Key issues/action forward- During one-to-ones, the manager should take some brief notes. Just a few bullet points will do. What you want to capture here are just the things you and your team member have agreed to do, and the key points you covered. For instance, you might have a few points like this:

- *We talked about how the time demand of your new training is affecting your workload, but it will end in two weeks' time and you will be back to full capacity.*
- *I agreed to review your training portfolio and sign off within a week of completion.*
- *You managed to get the new programme to work with 30% more efficiency by implementing the work-around you devised.*

You will want to make sure you aren't so busy scribbling on your notepad, or worse- with your nose in your laptop- that you give the impression you aren't actually listening at all. It can be really off-putting to be speaking to someone who is busy scribbling down everything you have to say.

It would be much better, after each discussion topic, to explain an awkward silence by saying "I want to be sure I capture this accurately" rather than be hunkered down with your pencil throughout the discussion. But with practice, you should be able to stay engaged, jot a few prompts for yourself, then flesh it out a bit when the meeting is over. You will get slick at this, and for all the time it saves in tackling performance issues and dealing with missed objectives later, you will be more than glad you did.

I know what you're thinking- you're a busy manager with a million things to do. No way should you be the one who takes the notes- that's for underlings, or even better, an admin person!

But here are the reasons *you* should fill out the form (and share it with your team member):

- It shows that you're listening, and it goes even further to show that you have heard what the person meant to say.
- It protects you in many eventualities- complaints, claims, and when making cases against ineffective team members.
- You can be clear about what needs improving, in your own words, and is written documentation in case there is no improvement.
- It acts as an active, ongoing staff development function that saves time and money later.

- It makes annual performance reviews much more meaningful, expeditious, and easy!

The one-to-one form template is in the workbook at the back of this book. You will also find a link to an online fillable pdf there.

Using this simple format, I was able to get biggest-hiring-mistake-of-my-career-Paula removed from the workplace. Our one-to-one forms showed all the times I had been specific about what she was doing (and not doing) that was putting her job at risk. The forms showed where she had agreed to do things differently following each meeting, with subsequent forms showing where no progress had been made. These records made all the difference to how fast and effectively I was able to complete her termination process, and stop her reign of terror over my team.

Most of the time, of course, these forms have a positive, constructive purpose.

In one department I took over, most of the technical staff had been working there for years under an ineffective director. This director hadn't kept the team's roles and salaries up to date with the national guidelines. After getting everyone's objectives rewritten and completing just a few months' worth of one-to-one forms, I was able to get them fairly graded with a market-rate salary based on the work they were doing.

When you document good performance, it shows those individuals that you recognise what they are doing, and it validates any reward or promotion they may get. It's great for retention and recruitment, too. Word gets around when a place is known to have supportive managers who listen, and help their teams improve.

If your organisation has any kind of governing body or board, they should be insisting that all staff have documented one-to-ones at least monthly. This protects them from all manner of claims, from negligence and malpractice to unfair dismissal, or even just from the dreaded 'she said, he said'.

This one-to-one process also fosters relationship-building in teams. You get to know each other better and faster with these regular catch ups. You can begin to easily see progress or slippage with consistent, documented discussions, which is great for conducting annual performance reviews.

Performance reviews: move your team forward (or rescue a struggling team)

I once took over a department that was so dysfunctional, no one could draw an organisational chart of the structure. A few attempts were made with the help of some of the staff that had been there the longest and those who were the most senior. The best effort looked like a plate of spaghetti. I had never seen anything like it in my whole career.

No one had up-to-date job descriptions or objectives, and you can bet there had been no regular performance meetings or reviews. I had no idea who had been working their tails off and moving the work forward, or who had been skating on the backs of their co-workers.

I didn't know who was good at what, and what work programmes were most effective. I didn't know anything.

It took everything I had not to just walk away from the job. It felt like an impossible task, and I was kicking myself for coming to work for an organisation that had let this happen. This was one of my first big lessons about the importance of conducting my own due diligence before signing on the dotted line.

I had to rebuild the department from the ground up. I had no idea where to start. I had moved to a new town, left a department full of people I had grown to respect and love, and moved away from good friends to take up this new challenge. I had no indication it was going to be like this, but I had given up too much to quit or fail. I had to suck it up.

The first thing I did was have each team member write up a set of no more than six broad objectives that they thought captured the work they were responsible for. My heart sank even further when I realised how many people had trouble doing even this first task.

In the meantime, I dug out my new organisation's annual reports and priority statements. I pulled together statistics about our local population's health needs, brought up national health programme guidelines, and wrote my own objectives.

Next, I needed to figure out how to get everyone from their current draft objectives to ones that supported mine and in turn the organisation's. This was where the one-to-ones really proved their worth.

I started with my senior managers. I explained the process and took them each through my objective-setting process in our one-to-one meetings. We also met as a team to make sure all our objectives read across as well as up. When we got to the point where we felt confident that they made sense together and standalone, I set my senior managers to work with their own teams.

They went back to their teams and repeated the one-to-one process with their direct reports, and so on through the department. Some of the staff, including those most senior, had never even had a face-to-face performance-related meeting with their bosses. It was a big culture shock to everyone, and I would be lying if I said it went quickly and smoothly. Some people adapted to it easily and appreciated the change. But there were plenty of others who had been very happy with their anonymity and autonomy to get on either with their own pet projects, or doing very little at all.

In fact, I found one man who had devoted his whole workload to addressing a rare condition that affected less than a handful of people in our community, just because a local politician's family was affected by it and they were pals. It wasn't even a condition that fell into our area of responsibility. His work was valiant, but misplaced.

Over the course of the first year, we used those monthly one-to-ones throughout the department to get the work up to standard, make sure everyone was clear on what they were supposed to be doing, and check we were on track to make the impact we were supposed to on the health of the local population.

Now it was time for the next big step: the first annual performance reviews. I had used the work on the objectives and the information that we were getting from the monthly meetings to draft a new organisational chart for the department. I knew I was going to have to make a case to the Board for a new budget, and request extra resources from HR in order to implement a big programme of change. Without performance reviews, this would've been impossible.

Performance reviews are a chance to look back over a year of work and check that objectives are still relevant and fit for purpose. But when you are looking at a programme of transformation, or having to make tough decisions about staffing, they become something even more valuable and worth many times over the time you put into them.

As for my new dysfunctional department, one year on, we used the outcomes of our performance reviews of all staff to:

- Create a new organisational chart
- Outline new job descriptions as necessary
- Make business cases for new roles and cases for eliminating some roles
- Create the department that we needed to in order to fulfil our purpose

Over time, conducting performance reviews with all staff gave me the evidence I needed to rebuild the budget for the department, get the support I needed from HR, and get it all signed off by the Board.

What's in a good performance review (and how to conduct one)

Not every leader will have to do the degree of whole-scale change and rebuild that I did. But, if documented one-to-ones and performance reviews can produce the credibility to do the transformation work I needed to, imagine the potential impact on a well-run and stable team year after year.

If you have kept up with the one-to-ones throughout the year, an annual performance review is a quick and simple exercise. There will be no surprises to you or the person you manage, because he or she will have been told all along what is working out well and what isn't.

It's also a very important time to see if the objectives that were agreed at the beginning of the year are still relevant, or if any priorities have changed (perhaps because circumstances in the department or in the organisation have changed). They can be updated and agreed on in the performance review.

It works. It makes a leader's life easier. It keeps team members engaged, comfortable with performance management, and confident they know where they stand.

In short, this system gives you the information you need for:

- Identifying professional development needs
- Evidence for bonuses, raises, and promotions
- Evidence for punitive action
- Evidence for programmes of change and requests for increases in budgets or other resources

The performance review template has these headings:

- Informal discussion
- Review of progress against objectives (to be completed by the team member prior to the meeting)
- Notes on achievement of objectives (to be completed by the manager)
- Workload review (to be completed by the manager)
- Professional development needs (to be completed by team member prior to the meeting)
- Key issues/action forward (for the manager to complete based on the discussion and shared with team member)

Informal discussion- Like in the one-to-ones, start the meeting with a general review of the year. Ask the team member to reflect on how they feel the year has gone, how they feel about their performance, and what the main challenges have been for them. This is a chance for a higher level, broad overview of a year's work, rather than the day-to-day of the previous month. If you have been doing your one-to-ones, nothing should come as a surprise in this conversation. If there are issues that come up that are unexpected, it is worth discussing why that might be.

Review of progress against objectives- Take each objective in turn. Notes on the degree to which the objective has been met should be completed by the individual before the meeting. They should have a chance to explain what they have written. You can talk together about those at which they have excelled, or those that they have struggled with. Acknowledge great work, especially when someone has gone above and beyond. Be sure to take time on those objectives where you and your team member have different views about whether or not the objective has been met adequately. Again, this should not be contentious or a surprise to either of you if you have been having your regular one-to-ones.

Notes on achievement of objectives- This is your opportunity to make your record of the outcome of the discussion about progress against each objective. Where the team member will have made notes about their progress in the section above, here you will record the outcome of your discussion about each one. You will note simply what you have agreed, such as *"You excelled at this objective and did some excellent work for the team"*, or *"Due to budget constraints it wasn't possible to fulfil this objective, but we will carry it forward"*. The value in this as an ongoing management tool is in its capacity to record performance. For instance, with consistent high performance, you may want to use this as evidence for a promotion or a raise. Likewise, regular notes about warnings that objectives have not been met give you scope to take punitive action.

Workload review- Following the informal discussion and discussion about objectives, much of the information about the overall workload will have come to light. Consider here if this person has too much on to be able to do their job well, or if it is causing stress. Alternatively, they may have additional capacity and want to learn a new skill that will contribute to the work of the team. Addressing this here and making a note of the discussion lets the team member know they have been heard. This is essential, especially if what they are saying is that they are overwhelmed by the amount of work they have to do. You may want to commit to supporting them to balance it either way. A record here protects you (and them) against any problems arising later, while helping you make sure you are getting the most out of your team.

Professional development needs- In this section your team member will have had the chance to reflect on their achievements and given some thought about whether any additional training or skill-building (such as a placement or secondment) might help them develop in their role. This may be in order to become a stronger team member or to develop their own interests. They have a chance here to make a case for this. You can discuss what is most beneficial to the team and what is a good investment in them as well. In the next section, you will record what you agree to support.

Key issues/action forward- Here you will record a few points on the outcome of the performance review. This should be what you and the team member have each agreed to do. Things like, *"You will research the best training course that will help you in your role and that fits into your work schedule"* or *"I will arrange for the information officer to take the cataloguing task from you to help balance your workload"*. Unlike the one-to-one actions, these are about setting up any major changes or points for the coming year. Then, the ongoing one-to-ones will support the achievement of these actions over the course of the next year.

The performance review form template is in the workbook at the back of this book. You can also get a full-size pdf version from my website at www.elizabethshassere.com.

If you only take away one thing from this book, let it be this...

There are many things in this book that I recommend you do as a leader, to create and build strong teams, improve overall performance and work-life satisfaction, and get a grip on challenging situations. But I would urge you that if you only do one thing, then that should be **implementing a consistent, documented one-to-one and performance management system**. The size of its positive impact on the state of your team and its value as evidence for all sorts of situations far outweighs the burden of its practice.

I know how busy leaders can be and how hard it is to make time for yet more meetings, particularly if you work in a highly bureaucratic industry. But managed well, you can have an adequate one-to-one in half an hour, and a stellar one in an hour, easy. If you directly manage so many people that scheduling even the briefest one-to-ones is impossible, you should think about breaking your team into smaller units with team leaders. It's important to have adequate oversight all the way through your team.

All those reasons you have for not conducting one-to-ones are dangerous myths. I have heard them all:

- Line management and supervision practices are only for micromanagers.
- It's unnecessary if you hire well.
- Staff hate one-to-ones and having their performance reviewed.
- It's time consuming and a burden of paperwork.
- It's a bureaucratic construct of limited or no value.
- It makes all parties uncomfortable, especially if the feedback is negative.
- In a small or informal office, such as at a startup or a company of young people, they are not appropriate.
- Only old baby boomers do that sort of thing, or government or bureaucratic institutions.

And many more...

I hope these few stories from my experience have given you some idea of how not only useful but valuable this practice can be. It really pays off in the long run.

Don't fall into the trap of thinking your team is the exception that doesn't require them.

In summary

- One-to-ones are essential for effective team building and are part of good leadership.
- Documenting one-to-ones provides evidence for a range of purposes that will save you time and headaches later.
- Good, documented one-to-ones provide all you need to conduct powerful performance reviews easily and expeditiously.
- Annual performance reviews based on one-to-one documentation gives you validated information for determining professional development needs, evidence for bonuses, raises or promotions, or punitive action.

These things are key to building a strong and united team.

In the next chapter

Now that you are building a strong, united team and have a standardised, scheduled, self-maintaining one-to-one and performance review process, let's look at how to troubleshoot, improve, and maintain it.

It's time to look at the four main building blocks for the foundation of your team. My simple four-part model will give you the framework to make sure all parts of your team are working as well as possible. It will help you find trouble spots or underlying issues that may be affecting performance as well as allowing you to quickly determine and implement solutions.

Chapter 3: How to identify what's broken and fix it fast: A simple four-part model that will give you the knowledge and control you need to become a fearless leader

"Everything should be made as simple as possible, but no simpler."
-Albert Einstein

Thanks to the sticky note termination, I was now in my first director job. I had taken over a department that had been mismanaged for years. Everything- from staff contracts to the offices to the finances- was a mess.

I was putting in ridiculous hours trying to sort everything out. It seemed that every problem I uncovered led to ten more; it felt like an impossible mountain that just kept growing.

It wasn't until I realised I was only seeing the forest and not the trees that I started to devise a way to tackle the problems effectively. I was trying to fix everything all at once while sitting at my desk, using just my brain. It finally dawned on me that there were a few fundamental issues that were creating the majority of the problems. Tackling those fundamental issues first would go a long way to fixing the myriad of other problems throughout the department.

Though I didn't yet have the benefit of years of running a good, slick one-to-one and performance review system, I knew I was building strong relationships with my team. My humility was starting to get my team onside and we were working together to improve things. But the challenges we were facing were huge. It was early days and I was still waiting for the tide to turn.

I was getting to know each person's skills and strengths through the one-to-one system. I figured we could work together to shed light on our toughest problems and find solutions to them. But I needed a way to make it feel manageable for all of us. I needed to give my team something tangible, like a framework, to grab onto. We needed to be able to control the flow of work and have a sense of accomplishment as we went along. I set out to get everyone on board and get stuck in to turning our department around.

Start with the model and an ally

Louise was my second in command. I was about six months in to this new role and we'd had time to get to know each other. She was a highly capable former nurse who took no prisoners and shared my frustration at the state of the department. She had been brought in just before I came on board to help the previous, struggling director. She was from the local area and knew the system we were working in well. The rest of the team immediately warmed to and respected her.

Where I had a strategic, big picture, problem-solving brain, she had an operational, practical, solution-finding one. We were a match made in heaven. If we could just get over our feeling of being overwhelmed, we could start to put some tactics to my strategy.

I had to delve into the depths of my brain to try and dig out some models and tools that I had learned throughout my training and career. I researched management analysis and leadership techniques, spoke to colleagues, and brainstormed with Louise. Everything I found was written in academic speak, was complex and time consuming, or assumed that I had lots of money at my disposal for expensive consultants to come in and do the hard work for us.

Then I came across a <u>personal development model</u> that was meant to help people find balance in and troubleshoot problem areas of their lives. It was made up of four simple areas that made practical sense to me:

- Spiritual
- Emotional
- Intellectual
- Physical

Could I apply this to a workplace environment? It turns out that these concepts fit perfectly. For the areas I'd had no idea how to start because it felt so complex and out of control, translating this model to the job at hand would break it down and make it manageable. It would be a much easier one to convey to the team than the jargon-filled ones I had found. I figured the last thing I needed to do was to impose an MBA-style academic exercise on everyone on top of the burden of chaos.

This is what happened:

- **Spiritual** became our **Mission Statement, Values and Goals**
- **Emotional** became the **Culture** of our team
- **Intellectual** became our access to and use of **Knowledge** (including staff skills sets) and **Information**
- **Physical** became our built **Environment**

I drew a chart that looked like this:

Personal development	Team development
Spiritual	Mission statement, values, goals
Emotional	Culture
Intellectual	Knowledge and information
Physical	Environment

I shared the model with Louise. She got it immediately. She improved my work with a few sharp suggestions and we began to discuss the best way to get all hands on deck to get it done. For the first time in months, with just one ally to prop up my hope, I felt like I could turn around the impossible disaster that was the current state of the department.

Get the rest of the team on board and put the model to work

Now, I will take you through an overview of the model and the process. In the chapters that follow, I will go into the detail of each of the four parts. I will show you how to work through each one.

All of the questions that are relevant to each part are in the workbook at the back of this book so you can go through everything you need to think about in each area. There are also full-size pdf worksheets available from my website at www.elizabethshassere.com.

Louise and I had thought carefully about how we should bring the rest of the team into the work we had planned. We figured it would be most effective to take a softer approach rather than run in on a Monday morning, throw the new model up on the wall and exclaim *"We're going to do all of this right now! Let's go!"*. Using specific pieces of work we were already doing, we would share our evolving thoughts on how we could make our transformation manageable for everyone.

We agreed that at the upcoming department meeting, we would introduce the plan to the team and get their input from the very beginning. We knew that getting them on board from the start was essential. We also figured there were people who could help us improve on it and come up with good ideas to make this model work even better.

Between Louise's work with our teams and our one-to-ones with every individual, we were quickly able to think about who we would get to lead on some of the first major tasks. We were also able to determine who might be best placed to get onside as advocates for the programme of work and plan out the rest of it to save us from drowning in the details. Besides, amidst all this, we still had our day jobs to do.

Applying the model is essentially about asking ourselves and others the right questions. That takes time, and some of that does need to be face-to-face. Of course, there will always need to be a balance between spending too much time in meetings and not having enough time together to make real progress. There is a temptation to get that cup of coffee and settle into a lengthy meeting analysing and rehashing every issue hoping they will magically get sorted through the talking, especially when the work is tough and people are feeling overwhelmed.

It is worth putting in the effort to get the balance right, though it can be tricky at first. Spending time together physically is important for creating a constructive culture and setting values. It helps to remind you all that you are doing this work for each other- the whole team- and that no one's work sits in isolation. The course of natural discussion and bouncing ideas off each other can be a great way to solve problems and come up with innovative solutions for change when there are complex issues to tackle.

Of course, there are many ways to communicate that don't involve sitting in a room together for hours. It's essential to explore those as well, especially if you have remote working or peripatetic team members. If you don't use these already, explore some <u>team collaboration tools</u> for keeping the momentum and communication levels up on projects.

But just like with one-to-ones, that face time is important, especially for new or developing teams. It is essential for creating the strong relationships that are required for doing tough, complex work. It requires everyone to be committed to it and to each other.

With the team on board, I started to work through the following questions:

Four parts of the model	Questions we began to ask ourselves and each other
Mission statement, values, and goals	• What is our overall mission? • What do we come in to do every day? • What are we striving for? • What do we want to achieve above all else? • How do we fit into the bigger picture (if we are part of a larger organisation)?
Culture	• What is it like to work here? • What does it feel like to be a part of this team? • Who does it appeal to (both staff and clients/customers)? • How are we perceived by the outside world?
Knowledge and information	• What skills are we missing in our team? • Do we get to develop our technical and professional skills here? • Do we have the information we need to do our jobs well? • Is it easy to access and to use?
Environment	• Is this a comfortable and functional place to work? • What would make it better? • How does it feel when we walk in the door every morning?

Each of the four parts has a more extensive set of questions applied to it, which are in the workbook at the end of this book. They are there to help guide your thinking. Some will be essential to your team and the work that you do, whereas others may not be relevant. No doubt you will also come up with many of your own questions as you go.

Using the four parts of the model to ask the right questions about the department made the problems fall in to manageable categories. It helped me to see the whole picture in a way that made it less overwhelming. I was now able to:

- Articulate my vision about where I wanted to take the department
- Analyse where there were key problems
- Prioritise those problems

Perhaps most importantly, it gave me a clear way to communicate these things to my team and get their input.

This is the process that worked for me:

1. **Apply the questions** in each element critically and openly to your team and your unique situation. I recommend that you, as the manager/leader, go through this on your own first, even if you are brand new to the job and your knowledge is very limited. At this point it is a simple **desktop exercise**. You may miss things, but in time, any blind spots will be filled by staff who have the organisational knowledge through length of service.

2. Using what you have come up with through your desktop exercise, **decide what is most urgent and important for your team's situation**. Think about your team members and who has responsibility for, or is the most knowledgeable about, these areas. Start a conversation with these people, your first line team, in order to get the rest of the team involved.

3. **Introduce the process and get people on side.** Choose your strategy with your first line team. Ask them to help you understand the problems you have identified and to come up with solutions for them. This is where the lessons in humility really come in handy! And this is just the start. How the rest of the team is engaged at this point will determine how

efficiently and effectively you get through the bulk of the work.

Many team members will be keen to have their say and to be a part of improving things. Others will be threatened by change and believe that any exercise to troubleshoot and improve is an excuse to get rid of people or make painful efficiencies. The way you manage your messages and relationships with your first line team at this point is key. Create shared messages and keep united.

I now had a guide which gave us all a much better sense of not only where we were going, but where we were starting from. It gave the team (and me!) hope that things could be improved.

As the leader, it boosted my confidence. Instead of running around in circles when I got overwhelmed with the size of the job of 'fixing' the department, I was able to take a breath, assess the situation based on the model, and consider how to engage my team. It meant I could get on with sorting things out.

This model went on to serve me well throughout the rest of my career. I got a reputation for being able to transform large, problematic departments. It helped me to turn around two more in my career, including managing major programmes of organisational change.

In summary

- Having a simple framework, or model, can help make an overwhelming situation more manageable so that you can get started troubleshooting and resolving any issues you find.

- This four-part model covers the foundational elements of a team, to help you focus your attention on the basic building blocks so that you can take control and get your team performing well.

In the next chapter

A mission statement is essential for building a united team that works well together and is focused and effective. It is the first and most important part of the model. I will take you step by step through a process for creating a great mission statement that best reflects your team's purpose. You will also find examples and sources to help you write a powerful statement that your whole team can get behind.

Chapter 4: Why creating a mission statement is the most important thing you'll ever do

"Mission statements [...] have a purpose. The purpose [is] to force management to make hard decisions about what the company [stands] for. A hard decision means giving up one thing to get another." - Seth Godin

I sat at the meeting table trying not to stare in panic at the five people who were looking everywhere but at me or each other. To say it felt awkward is a massive understatement. We were in deep trouble before we even started, and all of us looked like we would rather be having a root canal than be in this room.

I had pulled out all the stops. There was a full spread of food to get us through the morning- cakes and pastries, fruit, juice and coffee- but my senior management team were acting as if I was offering them poisoned tripe.

I reminded myself of what I had learned from speaking to a few colleagues and some peers working in partner organisations. Their previous director had been a notorious tyrant and a bully, and from what I could gather, no one would have been surprised if he had indeed brought in poisoned tripe for lunch. These people sitting at the table in front of me had previously been his 'whipping boys'.

I decided that my best bet was to be as humble and honest as possible. I talked about the things that were most important to me as a leader, such as integrity and transparency. I was clear that I knew that I succeeded or failed based on how well I created an environment that let them get on with their best work. I was adamant that I wanted us all to succeed, to enjoy our jobs, and get fulfilment from them as we did so.

I didn't hold back, though, when I talked about the challenges we faced. Major legislative changes on a national scale were going to change the way our profession operated. I also acknowledged that I could already see the appalling state of the department's administration, which had been seriously neglected by the previous director. Our ability to get things done would depend on sorting out the basic foundations first and foremost.

What I was talking about here was our **mission**, and I was doing this by letting my new team know what my **values** were as a leader. I also made it clear we had some very challenging **goals** to set.

I knew it was not going to be as easy as a rah-rah speech to suddenly transform this traumatised and neglected team of highly trained professionals into a powerhouse of resilience and industry, but I knew we had to start somewhere. I figured that agreeing- in writing- what was important to us to achieve and how we would get there was essential to a solid start.

A mission statement is the best place to start

The first part of this model is the most important element in your team's foundation. It involves determining your mission statement, establishing your values, and setting your goals. It comes first for four very important reasons:

- It sets the scene for all that you do as a team.
- It sets you up to do the work on the next three parts of the model.
- It's perhaps the easiest and least threatening task for your team members.
- It's a good exercise to begin engagement especially with a new team, whether it's you or they who are new to the job.

The term "mission statement" can sound a bit like something you may only need if you are an undercover operative or an astronaut. But I think renowned entrepreneur Seth Godin puts it best in the quote at the top of this chapter: your mission statement is a guide that helps you make tough decisions, particularly when deciding what *not* to do.

For me, a mission statement lets my team and I state in writing what is most important to us collectively. We cannot do everything, and a mission statement helps us stay focused. Many of us have particular interests or enjoy pet projects, but they may not be part of the priorities that we have all identified as necessary to meet our overall goals. It's good for the whole team to have a constant reminder of why we get up everyday to come and do what we do.

Forcing yourself to make hard decisions about what is and isn't important in your work is essential to leading an effective team. What you decide not to do is just as important as what you prioritise; it shows the world what your team stands for. When all team members understand and agree with your mission statement, focus, performance, and morale improves.

Don't try and tackle this alone; develop your mission statement with your team. It requires a thorough, well-led conversation about what is important to all of you. It also forces you to create some parameters, and there can be some good debates about what doesn't make it into the statement.

If you do it alone, you will struggle to get everyone signed up to it in principle as well as in practice. That's why I sat at that table with my senior team, surrounded by snacks, and forced myself to have the frank conversation with them about where we were, and how far it was from where we needed to be.

The magic of the mission statement and all that it gives you and your team

Here's a reminder about the context of this first part of the model:

Personal development	Team development
Spiritual	*Mission statement, values, goals*
Emotional	Culture
Intellectual	Knowledge and information
Physical	Environment

Creating a mission statement, describing values, and setting goals brings people together into a cohesive and effective team. In turn, this increases productivity and morale. Not doing the work here opens you up to competing priorities, wasteful action, and confused teams.

Your mission statement, values, and goals are the spiritual guide to your team and its work. Setting these out nails your colours to the mast. They are your flag flying, your logo emblazoned, and your journey-mapping for all to see. Without it, you and your team will be rudderless. That's why, as well as being first, I also consider this the most important element in this four-part model.

Spending time getting this right makes much lighter work of the other parts of your team's foundation. You will find that mapping back to your mission statement and goals ensures that you are on the right track with your work in the other areas.

Feeling aligned with what our team considers important can make all the difference to our individual performance. It gave our team a sense of inclusion and commitment that improves morale and positively affects culture. (We will explore culture in the second part of the model.)

There is power in writing your mission statement in plain language. This way, it's easy for all staff to get signed up to it (or not!), and their work can be held to account in alignment with it. Plus, what is written down can be discussed and negotiated, ensuring everyone feels like they have ownership of the purpose.

It also means staff have clarity and confidence in how their specific job supports the work of the department and the organisation as a whole. No matter the complexity of the work you do, your mission statement should be distilled down to the very essence of your business. Everyone, from the highest to the lowest level in the structure, should be able see how what they do every day contributes to moving the company forward.

Learning from the greats

The point of a mission statement is not to cover all bases and set out the entire mandate for the company. It should be a simple description of why your organisation or team exists. Let's start by looking at the mission statements of some big name companies:

To organize the world's information and make it universally accessible and useful. -Google

Build the best product, cause no unnecessary harm, use business to inspire and implement solutions to the environmental crisis. -Patagonia

Our vision is to be earth's most customer-centric company; to build a place where people can come to find and discover anything they might want to buy online. -Amazon

<u>Kaiser Permanente</u> exists to provide high-quality, affordable health care services and to improve the health of our members and the communities we serve.

If there are companies or organisations in your industry that have mission statements that you can relate to, there is no shame in starting with those. As long as what you end up with feels authentic and accurate, there is no need to try and create something truly unique. For a bit of creative inspiration, here is a <u>website</u> dedicated just to listing mission statements by industry.

It's a good exercise to start with the people who you directly manage to brainstorm the first draft. Throwing out key phrases is a quick way to get started.

For instance, when my team and I sat around the table surrounded by snacks that awkward morning, we got started with some real basics:

"protect the health of our population"

"promote programmes for healthy lifestyles"

We knew we needed to include *how* we were going to do these things, so we came up with a few phrases like:

"use commissioning processes that get the best value for taxpayers' money"

"by targeting the biggest health needs that affect the most people".

"through evidence-based decision-making"

We quickly began to see a few key phrases that we could use to build our statement. Keeping it short was a challenge, but that is what made us work hard to distil to the very essence what our work was all about.

And this is what we came up with:

"To protect and promote the health of our population by making evidence-based decisions for effective programmes that make the best use of taxpayers' money."

It was just a first draft, but the discussions we had while trying to choose what to keep and what to leave out helped us to get to know each other and what we valued. The time spent building our relationships, along with being able to refer back to a pithy yet powerful statement, did more to help us survive the next few tumultuous years than anything else ever could have.

This is why creating a mission statement is the most important thing you'll ever do as a team.

Mission or vision: What's the difference?

It is easy to confuse a mission statement with a vision statement. This definition says it best for me:

*"A **vision statement** is a vivid idealized description of a desired outcome that inspires, energizes and helps you create a mental picture of your target. It could be a vision of a part of your life, or the outcome of a project or goal.*

... vision statements are often confused with mission statements, but they serve complementary purposes." –From: timethoughts.com

A vision statement is aspirational.

Here are the mission and vision statements from my company, Textocracy:

Mission statement:

We believe everyone deserves to have their voice heard in the services they use- whether they are a council tax payer, an NHS service user, or a customer paying for a service or product with their hard-earned money- and that we should make it as easy as possible for people to be able to do that.

Vision:

We want every public service, hospitality service, business, and event to have a Textocracy number. We want Textocracy to be the go-to service for ensuring everyone has chance to have their say in the services they use.

As founder and CEO, the vision reflects what I aspire to for my company.

A vision is important, and can have a powerful effect on a company's morale. But for the purposes of this practical model, I am focusing on the mission statement.

What if your team or organisation already has a mission statement?

If you are part of an organisation where the mission and values are established and explicitly stated, this exercise should be straightforward. Your team's mission statement, values, and goals should logically fall out of the corporate ones. Start first with the highest level of your organisation and consider your overall mission.

If your team is part of a bigger organisation that does not have a mission statement, and explicitly stated corporate goals and values, it may be a bigger piece of work to devise those for your team from scratch. The principles remain the same, however, and consideration of the overall corporate aims should be used as a guidepost.

If your team already has a mission statement of some kind, it may be time to give it a 'sense check'. Go through it with your team to make sure what is written down is still relevant. Your statement might be outdated or missing essential elements that may have emerged as your work has developed over time. Give it a tweak if necessary, or if it's good enough for now, leave it until you have worked through the rest of this model, then revisit it.

Once you've finalised your statement, it becomes much easier for your values and goals to be agreed.

Values support you in accomplishing your mission

A mission statement helps a team determine its priorities. Values drive how a team accomplishes its mission and reflect what is important in achieving them.

Values include essential principles you can all sign up to. Values can be quite subjective, but following the work you have done to this point they should be starting to emerge:

"we will work together to a common end"

"we will respect and support each other in our work"

"we will keep our environment positive and productive"

Zappos is a company famous for the importance it places on its core values. You can see their list of ten values here. Here are a few of my favourites:

- Embrace and Drive Change
- Create Fun and A Little Weirdness
- Pursue Growth and Learning
- Be Humble [remember this from Chapter 1?]

Your values aren't meant to be textbook corporate jargon. They should honestly reflect what is important to you and your team while getting the job done. With Zappos' values, it is easy to see that these represent *how* they want to achieve their overall mission: "To provide the best customer service possible". They want to achieve this by embracing and driving change, while pursuing growth and learning, and by being humble (among other things).

When I was working with my team to come up with our first mission statement, it was clear that because of the history of bullying and intimidation from the previous leader, I would have to approach this carefully.

I had to keep in mind that the level of trust in this team was practically nil, and even starting a discussion about values was going to be a cultural stretch that might cause my new team to retreat into self-protection mode.

After a bit of a break and lots of snacks to congratulate ourselves on coming up with our mission statement in record time, we got back to work. During that break we'd talked about everything except work. The team seemed able to catch up with each other about their personal lives for the first time in ages, and I was able to just sit and listen and get to know them all a little better. I shared some stories about myself as well, and I became more of a person and less of a 'director' to them. This helped ease us into the discussion about our values as professionals.

We were able to come up with these five values to get us started:

- We will work together with respect and support each other.
- We will make evidence-based decisions for programme design and spending commitments.

- We will be united in standing up for the population we serve.
- We will create an environment of professional development for all team members.
- We will operate our business with integrity and transparency.

We arrived at this list through good-old brainstorming on a whiteboard. Everyone was able to scribble their thoughts on the board for everyone to see. Then, we sat back and had a discussion about all the values on the board.

It was a powerful thing just to see what was important to our teammates in the room. Though almost all of the statements were irrefutable, we were able to boil them down to our top five. We did this by pooling together those that expressed the same sentiment but perhaps in different wording. Then, we dropped the outliers that few people could get behind.

It was a great way to get to know each other, while coming up with some core values to guide our work. We had a whole department to tackle once we left that room. Our new mission statement and values would go a long way in shaping the discussions with our teams and guiding that work.

Setting goals takes you from the abstract to the specific

Goals state where you are trying to go. They are specific destinations, which is different to the more abstract aspiration in your vision.

They will, of course, be SMART (Specific, Measurable, Achievable, Realistic, and Time-sensitive). Time-sensitive goals mean that they may need to change periodically as some are accomplished, or be updated to reflect changes in circumstances.

For instance, for my current company Textocracy, our vision is: "We want every public service, hospitality service, business, and event to have a Textocracy number. We want Textocracy to be the go-to service for ensuring everyone has a chance to have their say in the services they use." In other words, we want to be the first choice for anyone who needs our kind of service.

In order for that to happen, we needed to set out some specific goals that will get us there. Here are a few that are helping us achieve our vision:

- Sign up all 150 health watchdog chapters in England by successfully committing 30 chapters each year for 5 years to use Textocracy, through content marketing and industry connections demonstrating its value

- Sign up 20% of annual health service events to use Textocracy for real-time live evaluation in year one, adding an additional 20% year on year

So, back to my previous role- though I had a lot of sympathy for my team of senior managers and the trauma they had been through with their old boss, and although our discussion and progress on our mission statement and vision had gone surprisingly well, it all came a bit unstuck when we talked about goals.

The lack of leadership previously meant that they more or less had free reign to choose their own priorities and work programmes. They were working on pet projects and historical hold-overs that weren't in line with our value to use an evidence base to choose programmes that our population needed most. There had been no oversight or accountability for them for so long that their workloads had grown to serve their own interests.

Making decisions about what had to go was a sensitive and prickly chore. Keeping us focused on building goals that were aligned to our mission statement and values, which included the statement about always prioritising work based on evidence, saved us from failure in this task.

Some of our goals we eventually decided on included things like:

- Over the next six months, review existing programmes against the evidence base and priorities as defined by our mission statement and values.

- Ensure every team member in the department has a clear set of up-to-date objectives by the end of March.
- By the end of August, complete an evidence-based business plan to present to the Board for the coming year's work.

Setting goals also helps you go on to set each team member's objectives, starting with the leader's. We had a lot of fundamental work to do, given the state of neglect of the department. But we now had a road map with a north star to help us on our way.

The following year, our goals and objectives could shift from the rudimentary turnaround work into powerful, impactful work on progressive programmes to meet the needs of the population.

In summary

- The mission statement is the most important element in your team's foundation.
- Shared values help build a united team and provide a guide to how you achieve your mission.
- Setting goals gives everyone a clear way to plan their work.
- The objectives that fall out of them give managers a guide for keeping up with and reviewing performance.
- The mission statement, values, and goals are powerful messages for communicating with

partners about the nature of what you do and what is important to your team.

In the next chapter

Once your mission statement, values, and goals are agreed, your team can begin to coalesce and relax into their work. It's easier to make decisions and prioritise competing demands and you can use these messages to aid in recruitment and retention.

Your mission statement, values, and goals give you a framework to begin to look at the culture of your team. Culture reflects the emotional health of your team and plays a key role in its effectiveness.

Elizabeth Shassere

Chapter 5: Why culture matters to your team when it comes to getting things done

"It turns out that what actually separates thriving organizations from struggling ones are the difficult-to-measure attitudes, processes and perceptions of the people who do the work.

Culture defeats strategy, every time."
-Seth Godin

Louise, my right-hand-woman, was trying to describe to me that something wasn't right with the team, but she couldn't quite put her finger on it. She said it was feeling 'clique-ish', and interpersonal relationships were beginning to suffer. She told me about sniping matches that were starting up between the admin staff and the technical specialists. By now, I knew that if anyone could get people to straighten up and act right, it was Louise. So if she said there was something fundamentally wrong with the way the team was getting along, I had better pay attention.

At first, we simply resolved to be better at noticing what was going on to see if we could pick up on what was triggering some of the most contentious interactions. I felt like a bad detective, but I was also kicking myself for having dropped the ball on taking care of the culture of our department. Waiting until something has gone awry is not a good time to remember the importance of keeping the emotional health of the team high.

After some time just being mindful of what was going on around us and chatting with various team members, one major contributor to the problem became clear. I am still amazed at the size of the impact something that appeared so inconsequential had had on my team.

At lunchtime, higher qualified "technical" staff would eat at their desks, afraid to waste a moment to get their workloads under control. Staff working at lower levels would take time to get out of the office and run errands, get some exercise, or just a bit of fresh air. It was causing a wider divide between those people whose work was seen as 'important' (because they couldn't stop even for a quick lunch break), and those whose work was so 'irrelevant' that it didn't matter if they left it for an hour in the middle of the day.

Of course, in reality, this wasn't true. But it was creating an atmosphere of 'us' and 'them' that was driving a wedge between department functions that relied on each other to be effective.

Louise and I really struggled to get our heads around what our evidence was clearly showing us. It seemed like such a small and petty thing, but it was having a real impact. More to the point, we didn't want to admit to ourselves all the things we had perpetuated or overlooked in our own culture that were causing the problems.

Why did we think it was ok to create a culture where the only way to keep your head above water or to feel like your work was important was if you never got time for a break, much less a whole lunch hour? How did we neglect our admin staff to the point that their work was seen as less important by our technical staff? Why had we let a divide form between groups of staff, and to the extent that it was affecting how people felt at work?

There was plenty of time for self-flagellation later. First, we had to fix our broken culture.

Culture: what it means and why it's important

This second part of the four-part model involves determining the desired culture of your team, then making changes and improvements in order to achieve it. The culture in a team or organisation is set by the collective behaviour of individuals. Culture is the sum of the emotional intelligence of the group of people working together and what standards and values they adhere to.

Personal development	Team development
Spiritual	Mission statement, values, goals
Emotional	*Culture*
Intellectual	Knowledge and information
Physical	Environment

Culture is more complex than setting a mission statement. But once you have identified the mission statement and values of your team, it becomes much easier to create the culture you want for your team.

Culture is about how it feels to come in every day and give at least eight hours of your time to that organisation or team. Good, aligned culture boosts productivity; it creates the atmosphere you need for innovation and creativity. A poor or mismatched culture can completely undermine all that you are aiming to achieve.

Get your culture right and your organisation will have a great reputation that makes people want to work with you. Get the culture wrong, or ignore it altogether, and you can struggle to recruit or retain the people you want with the skills you need. Culture is spread by word of mouth by current employees to prospective talent. They may not be consciously talking about culture, but it is what they mean when they say things like "we are allowed to make mistakes and learn from them", or "we are not micromanaged", or "good informal mentoring goes on here". It creates your reputation as an employer and a manager.

That is why culture defeats strategy. The best business strategy in the world cannot save a team mired in a destructive culture.

How to get started

Assessing the existing culture in order to find out what is good and bad, or what is working well for team members and what they don't like, is relatively straightforward. But that doesn't mean it's easy. It requires a lot of talking, listening, and observing, all while you and your team are getting on with your day jobs. It takes a good deal of your own emotional intelligence and at times, subtlety, to analyse and positively impact your culture.

As the leader, the buck stops with you. You have the power and responsibility for making sure the culture is right for your organisation and that it is working for your team. But it is not something you can do on your own, especially if you manage staff who in turn manage their own teams. You will need to get everyone on side.

And if you, like me, aren't the greatest with emotional intelligence and feelings, even professional ones, you will need to bring in your best, most trustworthy people to be your eyes and ears. For instance, without Louise, there is no telling how long our clique problem would have brewed before I noticed. It probably would've been when it had blown up in my face.

If you are a new leader with a new team, getting other trusted people on board is even more important. Besides, no one can pick up on everything. Having a few people addressing the culture makes a much better job of it. Even peer leaders who are not managers can be very helpful in taking the emotional temperature of a team and assist in identifying the things aren't working for most people.

They will know and understand the history behind the current culture as well. Culture is often organically grown; it's made up of history and personal relationships (good and bad), a compilation of hiring mistakes, unchecked bad habits, and happy accidents.

Things like morale and sociability, motivation and atmosphere, are all important parts of culture. The way that your team chooses to do things and the processes and methods that are in place are also key factors. All of these things impact the way it feels to try and get things done, and therefore affect culture.

As Seth said in his quote at the beginning of the chapter, these things are *"difficult-to-measure attitudes, processes and perceptions"* of the people in your team. Talking about them helps bring them to light- you should give your team a straightforward way to comment on the culture and its positive and negative effects on their workday. Depending on the current state of the culture, you should be having open and honest face-to-face discussions. In small or tight-knit teams, this approach will get you a lot of information, fast. If the state of things is so poor that even a conversation is a stretch, give people an anonymous or written way to feed in their feelings about team culture. The important thing is to open up the dialogue, create an atmosphere that welcomes people to safely share their observations, and commit to taking action to improve things.

There are an extensive set of questions at the back of this book to guide you through starting a conversation about culture. You will also find a link to a fillable pdf there.

Once you've opened up the conversation, either in person or by some other method that gives people a place to make their comments, you should begin to see repeated issues that show a pattern or raise consistent concerns across the team.

You might see a mix of positive and negative comments, such as:

"Every Tuesday, when all the managers go out to lunch, it feels like the rest of us are being excluded just because our jobs aren't as important as theirs. Can we designate a day for all staff to get together and have lunch with the managers, say, in the board room, so we can feel included and seen?"

"One thing I really look forward to in the week is when we get together to look at the numbers and see how much our hard work is paying off, no matter how small our contribution. It seems to make it all worth it. Let's not lose that, or maybe we can even do more of seeing the direct impact of what we each do that makes us all able to achieve the team's goals."

You might even be surprised at what comments on culture tell you about other problems you have noticed but couldn't see the connections. For instance, you might find yourself thinking, *"Oh, so that's why it seems nothing ever gets done on a Tuesday afternoon!"*.

By its very nature, doing the work on the mission statement, values, and goals first, then culture, can have a tremendous benefit to team cohesion. It often enables you to solve problems as you go along, saving the time and energy in implementing solutions later.

Actively working on this element will let *you* begin to define what your culture is, rather than relying on luck or fate. It will help you get to know your team better, understand how they operate, what is important to them, and what their biggest challenges are.

How observing, listening, then acting solved our 'clique' problem

Culture is an underlying current that runs through your team. Also, like a current in a river, it propels the work forward and feeds the motivation of the team. It's often invisible and has much more power than you can see on the surface. Like a dangerous undertow, not paying attention can get you swept out to sea. Louise and I quickly found ourselves uncovering even bigger staff problems within our clique problem. We needed to nip this one in the bud, fast.

Louise had been observing what was going on around her. Once she identified there was a problem and shared that with me, we began to make more of an effort to talk informally to our team. We simply asked them about how they felt about their jobs, about the workplace atmosphere, and any suggestions they had for changes and improvements.

What we heard let us know that we needed to make more of an effort to bring all levels of staff together. We wanted everyone to appreciate that every role played an important part in our work, and to see how what they did fit into the whole picture. We also wanted to scrap the perception that people should have to work straight through the day without a break in order to stay on top of their workloads. Even more importantly, we didn't want people to feel that, in order to be valued, they had to appear busy and overwhelmed.

We started by bringing people together once a week for an inclusive lunchtime session where each team in turn would showcase their work and explain how it fit into the mission and goals of the department. They might also describe a particular challenge they were facing and ask for help, or share upcoming changes that would affect others. These then became social events, with people bringing food to share and using the time to celebrate birthdays and holidays.

This practice went on to make a huge positive impact on the culture of the whole team.

The department became inclusive and supportive. That change in culture went on to help us weather some organisation-wide challenges in restructuring and leadership. This came from simply observing what people were doing throughout the day and seeing where the problems were. It didn't cost the department anything and didn't take up any additional time, but it went on to have a massive impact on just about everything we did.

In summary

- Once you know what the main issues are that affect the culture of your team, you can prioritise and address them.
- Opening up the conversation will get people thinking and talking about the attitudes, processes, and perceptions that are part of their every day working life and that are so important to culture.

- The first two parts of this model are quite conceptual and human nature plays a big part in them. This can make them difficult to quantify and predict.
- Doing this work is more than worth the effort that goes in for the return in productivity, improvements in the workplace, and the benefits for the individuals in your team.

In the next chapter

The work you will have done on your mission statement, values and goals, and culture, has set you up for the next two parts of this model.

Knowledge and information and **Environment** are complex areas but are much more practical in nature. I find working on these two areas particularly satisfying. They have tangible elements in which you can quickly see the work that you have done starting to make improvements in the everyday functionality of your team.

Chapter 6: Knowledge and Information: How getting the balance just right gives you a competitive edge

"We are drowning in information but starved for knowledge." -John Naisbitt

The director from whom I was taking over this department had been asked by the chief exec to stay on for some handover time. In our first meeting, I asked her for a copy of the department organisational chart.

She replied, *"Well, it's not quite done yet, I'm still working on it."*

"That's ok, I just need to see where we stand so far, then I'm sure I can work with the team to finish updating it."

"Well, we are having to start from scratch, see, we didn't have one before you asked for it."

"?...."

"It's proving a bit difficult."

"?!?!?!"

"See, it's quite complicated...."

>regaining my composure< *"Let me see what you've got."*

She scrabbled through a giant, messy sheaf of papers in her bag. She pulled out a dog-eared and tea-stained A4 sheet. At first I thought she must have grabbed the wrong one. It was just a Pollock painting of multi-coloured boxes, splattered across the sheet with squiggly lines running between them in no discernible pattern.

"See, we have some complex relationships as we have been doing without some key skills for a while. We've had to do a bit of doubling up."

She seemed almost proud that she had not only managed this 'doubling up', but that she had just about managed to capture the pesky thing on paper, like capturing a butterfly under a glass.

With all the other things I was uncovering about the management of this department, I really shouldn't have been surprised. But there was something fundamentally wrong about her not being able to represent in an org chart what staff she had and who managed whom. In that moment, I just wanted to run screaming from the office and go back to my old job. I could hear my old boss laughing maniacally and shouting *"No backsies!!"*.

When taking over this department, the org chart was just one of the useless (or even missing) pieces of information I uncovered.

This little encounter with the ex-director told me:

- There wasn't adequate skill and knowledge in the department to run things to any sort of common standard, including an appropriate reporting structure.

- There was not enough value placed on documentation, written information, and record-keeping of some of the most basic things necessary to keep a team functioning properly.

It was time to take a deep breath, shake out the carpet, and see what falls out. It looked like I was going to have to pick up the pieces and rebuild the department from the ground up.

Taking stock of your knowledge and information increases productivity

This third part of the four-part model is the key to the effectiveness of your basic operations. Knowledge and information includes a comprehensive list of all the components that allow you and your team to practically get your work done.

Personal development	Team development
Spiritual	Mission statement, values, goals
Emotional	Culture
Intellectual	*Knowledge and information*
Physical	Environment

This part of the model corresponds to the idea of the intellectual self- how you use information and your innate skills to get on in life. You need some knowledge and skills, like how to cook or how to ride a bike, and you also need to know how to get your hands on essential information, like a phone number or a mortgage application. The same goes for your work.

Knowledge refers to your staff skill sets- the knowledge your team has to have in order to do their jobs properly, as well as any qualifications or training required to do them effectively. Information refers to the data and information that your team must have to perform their work to the highest possible standard, to keep that competitive edge, as well as operate safely (depending on your industry).

Information in its broadest sense includes financial information, which is a powerful tool for your business. Forensic analysis and monitoring of financial performance helps you tweak your management decisions for the best possible outcomes.

This is the Goldilocks part of the model in that your access to knowledge and information should be just right. Too little information and you can't make good decisions and do the right work well. Too much or badly disorganised information and you spend too much time swimming through it trying to discern what is useful (while losing productivity in the process).

Too little knowledge in your teams and your performance suffers. Too much knowledge, or expensive skills sets that aren't necessary, and you are costing yourself more money than will give you return on your investment.

But getting the balance isn't a dark art. It's easy once you take stock of what you have. First, you need to create a map of your team's functions and think critically about what you do and what you need in order to do it.

How creating a functions map for your team will help you in everything you do

As I sat with my head in my hands, staring at the modern art that was supposed to be the organisational chart for my new department, I wondered how I was ever going to make any sense of who did what. I figured I would have to start with one loose end and pull, like unravelling a knitted jumper.

I decided to start by mapping our service through an annual business cycle.

At the beginning of the year, we received annual statistics on what was causing the most ill-health and early deaths in the population. We would design our programmes to meet the population's needs. We would put this together into a business plan and submit it for the Board's approval. Then, we had to actually deliver the services and react to unplanned demands (such as health emergencies or politicians raising an issue out of the blue).

I also needed to consider all the administrative functions that almost any department requires just to keep the wheels on: ordering office supplies, processing human resources forms, making sure the place is cleaned, and so on.

Using a methodical and super-practical approach to functions mapping which I describe step by step below, I was able to throw away the org chart of spaghetti. I could start fresh and begin to build what we needed.

1. **Start by mapping the functions your team are required to perform.** It's important here to put aside any existing job descriptions and the individuals who are currently doing those jobs. This can be hard, but if you begin by mapping by person, your biases for those you personally like, or who do awesome things but that perhaps aren't priorities, will creep in. Your objectivity will go out the window and you will have wasted your time. You should only be thinking about *what* needs to be done, and don't worry about by whom yet.

2. **These functions will each have a required skill set, qualification, or training. List next to each function what those things are.** You may need someone with a specific electronics certificate, or someone who speaks Spanish. Other jobs may require a broader range of skills, such as office software, reception skills, and customer service.

3. **Next, go back through and map your existing staff to those functions.** Be sure not to forget yourself in this exercise. Consider the staff that you have on your team and the skills and knowledge they need to do these jobs.

It will serve you well to complete a functions map now for your team. It gives you a helpful guide against which to consider the work you will do with the rest of the model. You might want to choose to map through an annual cycle, a financial year from start to finish, or a project or product management cycle. It doesn't matter; what is important is that you give yourself a guide to make it as easy as possible to capture all the functions that your team performs.

Knowledge, skills, and getting things done

Many teams grow organically over time, so the gaps and gluts that come to light when we sit down and map out what we have in our teams can be surprising.

Making sure that your team has the right skill sets is essential in order for it to run effectively and efficiently. Matching in-house skill with the required functions is a straightforward way to analyse where the gaps are. A deficit in this area can give your competitors the edge they need to outperform you (or result in poor outcomes for your team).

Struggling along without the right skills in your team creates a strain on everyone involved. It can be demoralising for those who are trying to pick up the slack or make do without much-needed input, which can have a negative impact on the culture of your team.

Once you've identified the gaps, think about whether any existing staff could be upskilled, retrained, or redeployed. When people have long-standing organisational knowledge and memory, or when they simply fit well in the team and the culture, it's better to keep them around, if possible.

Skills can be pooled or shared, too. For example, one person may be able to perform a certain function for everyone, freeing others to spend more time on a more lucrative task that benefits the company.

This kind of investment in people improves morale, retention, and performance in teams. And all these things are part your culture. Getting this right pays off in spades!

It's important to include staff in this process, too. Reviewing skills and functions can be a red flag to teams who might immediately think that you are carrying out an exercise to make cuts or decide who is redundant. If that is your purpose, work with your other managers, or your peer leaders to manage that message honestly and sensitively. That is not what this part of the model is about here, though. This is about managing the resources in your team better and getting the most out of individuals (and your budget).

Here's an example of how it worked for me

We used to get half a dozen electronic newsletters every day from various public health-related agencies. Most of them would include government policy updates and best practice recommendations that would directly affect our programmes and their design. The problem was, it was a real burden for staff to try and sift through to find what was relevant to their areas of responsibility. Someone working on obesity programmes didn't need to know the details about flu prevention campaigns, for instance.

I had an admin officer who had a degree in research methods but wasn't using it. Once I discovered this, I put those skills to good use. I redeveloped her job description to include cataloguing and summarising the information in the newsletters as they came through.

She made short work of clustering the information into one weekly digest for everyone. Each person could then jump easily to the topics they needed to know about. Problem solved!

Though that person began to cost us a bit more money in salary from her re-graded job description, the time she saved our expensive technical staff more than made up for it. They became more effective and efficient at implementing the latest public policy, and she was getting to use her hard-earned skills and thriving in her new role.

Supporting existing staff to develop skills and grow professionally benefits morale and boosts your team's reputation (and it makes good business sense!). This sort of culture is highly sought after by those good hires you may be looking for.

Getting the balance of information right for better productivity

The story of our re-purposed admin officer takes us nicely into the second half of this part of the model, **information**.

Staff must not only have access to the information they need, but it has to be manageable, so as not to waste time in their search for what is relevant. In this age of instant access and constant feeds, the ability to quickly sift what is valuable and important from what is not is essential.

Of course, it is not just the quantity of information that is the issue here. You can have access to huge hauls of data, for instance, but it might not be the most relevant or of a sufficient standard for your team to do their job well. People can feel devalued and demotivated when they struggle to get the tools they need to do their best work. If this is a constant battle, it can have a detrimental effect on morale and in turn, culture and productivity.

Then, you also need to have an efficient system for handling the information you have. Like our need to get a handle on dozens of health policy bulletins a week-though it was great information, we just didn't have a system that let us get the most out of it.

An investment in higher quality data or a better way to manage information might just give you the competitive edge you need to overtake the competition, or simply improve the quality of your service. The better you are at managing your information, the more effective and efficient your team will be.

Getting the balance of access to and management of information right will save you money in the long run and increase your whole team's productivity, innovation, and problem-solving ability.

Mapping your information needs

Most jobs require access to some sort of dynamic information. Few of us can work without regularly updated guidelines, the latest research results, or market reports and articles. Finding exactly what you need can often mean swimming through a deluge of useless information. You need to be able to search effectively without spending an inordinate amount of time doing it.

The best way to discover your team's information needs is to ask them. They will be able to quickly and easily tell you about their own information challenges. They live them daily, and should be able to recite those things that cause them the most delay and frustration.

People react positively to being asked to think about and record the things that cause them problems if it means that solutions can be found. Many will have had ideas about this for a while, but may not have felt there was the appetite or opportunity to share them with the team and to find a way to implement them.

If you have done your function mapping to determine necessary skill sets and staff, you can more easily map what information each of these functions (and therefore individuals) need in order to do their jobs well.

There are two issues here that you will be troubleshooting: 1) getting the information you need without having too much to deal with, and 2) having an effective and efficient system in place for handling and managing the information you have.

Just like with knowledge and skills, it is important to spend some time analysing what information and data you have and what you need. Then, you'll need to determine the gap between the two. Once you have done that you can figure out how you will fill the gap.

Over the course of a month, get every member of your team to do this exercise:

- Every time they are in the flow of working and they find themselves scuppered or slowed down by not having some data, information, or intelligence at their fingertips, have them write it down.
- Every time there is a problem with the system of handling information that prevents them from working or that slows progress, have them write that down, too. This could be a process that gets stuck because it relies on one person who goes off sick, or a bureaucratic approval process needed for access.
- At the end of the month, run a workshop where you pool what you have each written down.
- After grouping the common issues, take out any duplication.
- Identify the information that the team needs that you don't get now.
- Map the flows of information and highlight where people have noted problems in the system with process and access.
- Brainstorm some solutions. If some problems are too complex for this, get some people on board who are willing to go away and work on finding a way to solve them.

Once you've sorted out your information flows and access, keep checking with staff regularly. Over time, access to information may change so subtly that you don't realise when you start to struggle to get what you need to keep up with new demands, or when output starts to slow down because your sources have outgrown the efficiency of your system again. Regular check-ins will help to avoid this drift.

Financial information isn't just for the finance team

I stood in a daze at a long meeting room table with spreadsheet upon spreadsheet laid out like a numerical tablecloth. I felt like screwing it all up throwing it into the bin. I could not for the life of me see where the pot of money was, but I knew it was there. It must be, because payments were coming out of it, on a regular basis.

I really shouldn't have been surprised. I had already found three people being paid by us that were working at another agency. There were no employment contracts that matched those salary line items. I thought I must have been losing my mind. It couldn't really be this bad, could it?

Every single public sector department I took over had finances in as bad a state as this. Outdated or missing information, historical contracts being paid when the work had long stopped, you name it. I was astounded by the lack of transparency and commitment to basic documentation. Simply unpicking the funding streams and allocations took months, never mind actually fixing the problems I found.

Finances had been allowed to run year after year based on historical activity. No one was watching for drift, or aligning staff changes against contracts, or programmes that had ended against automatic payments. It was neglect, plain and simple. The organisation hadn't gone bust, so the money just kept flowing. The level of waste was a tragedy.

Mapping your finances for smarter decisions and better business

Financial information may seem like a no-brainer and you may wonder why it is in here at all. Especially in larger organisations, you will have whole finance functions whose responsibility it is to manage your financial information.

As a director or manager, it's easy to think that as long as you are staying in budget then your operations are fine. But the detail behind your financial activity can tell you a great deal about the performance, effectiveness, and efficiency of your team. Knowing what you have, how you spend it, your return on investment, and the proportionality of your expenditure is key to better management, better decision-making, and better planning.

If you don't keep on top of the financial reporting and analysis of your budget, you could find yourself spending a disproportionate percentage of your money on an aspect of your work that is not providing a great enough return to warrant that expenditure.

Therefore your 'database', or library of information, should include a forensic provision of financial intelligence. Just like subject matter intelligence, this information keeps the functions running efficiently, and prevents certain categories of expenditure from rising or falling so incrementally that the changes go unnoticed until it starts to have a real impact on your business.

Since you've already mapped your functions to determine your skill and information needs, adding a financial activity to this analysis is straightforward. This is different to simply keeping a balanced budget, or bookkeeping.

Depending on the size of your team and your structure, you may have one or a small team of individuals who can take on this exercise and pull a picture together of the distribution of spending across your team. This can then form the basis of a conversation with the whole team about where changes may need to be made.

Some issues may be obvious, such as spending lots of money on hard copy trade journals when an electronic subscription that all staff can access would be cheaper (and greener!). You may also reveal some subtleties, for instance, that the money you are putting into newspaper ads is giving you little or no return.

It can be easy to downplay the importance of doing this work comprehensively if you have a balanced budget and finance officers who have overall responsibility for the books. But unless your team has money to burn, it is more than worth taking a comprehensive look at how your money is allocated.

Doing this work is a valuable exercise in bringing the team together, helping you to think about your values and goals and what is important to you as a team. When everyone has a view of the overall financial profile of the business, it impacts the way they conduct their own activity and improves their understanding of how their work fits into the whole.

Being open and transparent across your team about its finances also has a positive impact on the culture. People feel trusted and engaged, and will have a better understanding of how their work contributes to everything that you do.

In summary

- Working on knowledge and information in a considered and analytical way can save you time and money, build a stronger team, and improve your culture.
- Starting with mapping your functions, skills, and information helps you understand your business forensically. This gives your team the power it needs to excel rather than just survive.
- This process can mean the difference between weathering challenges or collapsing under an unexpected strain.

In the next chapter

At this point you will have set out a clear position for your team, including its mission statement, values, and goals. You will be building a strong and united team through regular one-to-ones and performance reviews. And, you will have got to grips with the details that make up the foundation of your team's work- the knowledge and information that makes it all happen. Doing the work on knowledge and information may lead you on to a whole new way of thinking about your business, your performance, and how you measure and improve everything that you do.

In the next chapter, I will take you through the most important thing you'll never notice, which will pay you back in dividends when you start to give it some attention: the physical environment in which your team works.

Chapter 7: Why your team's physical environment is the most important thing you'll never notice

"[The building you work in] is a culture and values issue worth fighting over."
-Steve Blank

There was black and green mould growing in the corners of almost every room. The large meeting room was the worst; it also had bubbling plaster and a crumbling window frame. The stairs weren't square or level. They leaned and drooped from floor to floor. Just walking up them made me feel drunk. I was assured it passed all health and safety and fire codes. "I'll take it", I said to the Head of Buildings and Maintenance.

I had just agreed to move my whole department into this dilapidated and smelly space. That's how desperate our accommodation issues were, and how badly they were affecting our ability to work.

Good managers notice the environment

The fourth and final part of this model is all about the **environment** in which your team works. Don't be fooled by its position last in the model; it has tremendous potential to influence your team and all that it does. The quality and characteristics of the workplace are the first things that affect people when they walk into the building each morning to go to work, even if they don't realise it.

Personal development	Team development
Spiritual	Mission statement, values, goals
Emotional	Culture
Intellectual	Knowledge and information
Physical	*Environment*

This part of the model correlates to the idea of the "physical self". Just like our physical self, we must think about how we develop and maintain our space in order to function as we need to. I may strive to be a champion runner, but if I don't get my body into the proper condition, it's not going to happen. If I want to foster relaxation or the ability to entertain a big extended family at home, having a chaotic or tiny space with a small table and a few chairs just won't cut it. The physical environment has a great deal of power to affect what goes on in that space, much more so than we are often aware.

Whether or not people are comfortable at work sets the context for everything else they do. Anything else they may be looking forward to or dreading- such as a new project or a boring meeting- is in the context of a specific environment that has an impact on how they feel about it.

Not convinced yet?

Imagine that you have put on some very tight trousers, shoes that are two sizes too big, a thick, woolly jumper and bobble hat before going to work in the middle of summer. You would probably find yourself so uncomfortable that you couldn't sit and focus or concentrate on what you were doing. You would be distracted by your floppy shoes that wouldn't stay on your feet, you would be boiling hot and probably sweating buckets, and the itchiness of the bobble hat would be driving you mad. To say the least, your productivity would be close to nil. More importantly, you would most likely get very grumpy and not be at all in the mood to work well with your colleagues.

Of course you're not going to go to work dressed for an Arctic expedition, but it does illustrate the impact that the physical comfort dictated by the physical environment can have on your team.

Now imagine it is your workplace, and not your clothes:

You're an administrative officer such as a secretary or receptionist, and you have to sit at your desk for nearly 8 hours a day with little or no chance of ever leaving that environment. Your chair is old and uncomfortable, and doesn't adjust to suit your size.

You are in the very draughty foyer of an old Victorian building with wind blowing through the ill-fitting window and an external door that gets stuck open every time someone walks in or out. You are constantly having to get up and close the door. The walls are dingy yellow and peeling. There is a ring of green and black mould growing just around the base of the wall behind you where you have to stash your bag and coat.

The noise levels in the foyer are extreme; there are no soft furnishings or carpet, and there is a well-travelled path that runs right across the front of your desk. You find yourself answering every query from every passer-by. You're asked for change for the vending machine, told that the ladies' room is out of toilet roll, complained to about the way a worker in another building treated them, and blamed for the failings of the new one-way system around the grounds.

To say your productivity would be severely hindered by this environment is quite an understatement. You may not even realise it, but your mood and stress levels might be through the roof, affecting both your mental and physical health. Your colleagues may complain about how unpleasant you are, how inefficient you are, and how you never seem to get anything done. It may even affect whether or not you keep your job.

All these things come from just a few physical attributes of the space in which this person sits every single day for 8 hours a day, five days a week. No manner of mission statements, Christmas parties, compliments or other rewards are going to change the fact that this member of staff sits in this same miserable environment all day every day.

Get these three things right in your environment and see results

This part of the model assumes you work in an office building of some sort, and not on a fishing trawler or on an assembly line in a factory. By office building, I am referring to a space that allows for working at desks or tables, that is indoors, and has a built, static structure- whether it's a traditional office, a house, a loft, or a converted barn.

I do, however, like to think that the concepts and principles laid out here, including the questions that can be addressed to improve things, are valuable in the most unusual of working environments.

The physical environment is often disregarded or left ignored on the bottom of the priorities list. This is usually for two reasons: 1) either trying to tackle your built environment feels too big or out of your control, or 2) you simply don't recognise just how much of an impact it is having on your team's working life. This is a mistake.

If you have a problem with staff sickness levels, poor performance, low morale, or poor staff retention, it could be at least in part down to the physical space you all work in.

The effects of the physical environment can be quite insidious; we can often be negatively affected by our physical surroundings without even realising it. Sometimes we get used to our environment and stop 'seeing' how things really are. Or, we are so busy or focused on *what* we are doing that we don't realise how the physical condition of *where* we are working is impacting *how* we are working.

Your team will have ideas about what the big issues are in your workplace that could use improvement. Ask them to observe what is going on around them. Little things will begin to show themselves, like having the supply closet on the other end of the building from the printer, and the time wasted traipsing between the two. More impactful issues may arise, such as business lost or delayed because there weren't adequate meeting facilities for clients, or adequate remote-working tools.

Physical environment problems can take on all sorts of characteristics. Some are quite small but have a massive impact. Can people make themselves a drink with minimal time away from their desk? Is the space clean and uncluttered? Do they end up having to wash mugs for five minutes before they can even start?

There are three main physical characteristics of the workplace, however, that should be your biggest considerations:

- Comfort
- Functionality and Organisation
- Equipment and IT

Comfort

If you are located in an older building, there can often be issues with poor temperature control, draughty windows, and odd space configurations.

Regardless of the age of the building, temperature, lighting, noise, and even smells are often cited as things people struggle with the most in getting comfortable in their workspace. This is important because whether consciously or subconsciously, the time spent fidgeting and adjusting trying to get rid of an annoyance or discomfort cuts into productivity and output. Moving chairs and desks to avoid a draft or get rid of a glare, adjusting a chair a dozen times to avoid a stiff neck, ranting (internally, of course) about the smelly lunch or over-abundant perfume from someone in the next cubicle- all these things begin to take a toll on your team's concentration, and frankly, can make a person downright miserable.

Functionality and Organisation

How your space is set up and organised is also important. For instance, both open plan and rabbit warrens of closed doors have their drawbacks with regards to functionality as well as atmosphere and morale.

When an office is open plan, people will often complain about noise and space constraints. Human nature often dictates that even when a space is supposed to be fluid and hot desks claimed each day on a first-come basis, most people will gravitate to the same desk each and every day. People can get very tetchy if they feel like someone else has taken 'their space'.

But closed doors and private offices can make for an exclusive, isolationist environment that both perpetuates hierarchy and hinders communication.

Design options like open plan or closed doors have a significant, un-ignorable impact on morale, productivity, and general satisfaction at work. Of course, it doesn't have to be one or the other. These are powerful design choices that can perpetuate the culture you want.

The most important things to consider are your culture, functions, and budget. Determine what type of space is best for the work that you do and the type of company you are. Even if you have a beautiful, modern, and comfortable office, taking a little bit of time to analyse its functionality and how people feel about it can sometimes reveal a small thing that is having a disproportionate impact. For instance, is the printer too far away from the admin staff who use it the most? Only one drinks machine for too many people? You might be surprised when you discover the things that undermine the work that people should be doing (which, in turn, affects your business).

Equipment and IT

IT often presents one of the biggest challenges for teams and organisations. When it works it goes unnoticed and underappreciated. But when it stops working, everything can come to a standstill. It can become impossible to complete the simplest of tasks or communicate with others outside of the building.

When I worked in the public sector, IT was one of the biggest sources of frustration, lost productivity, and danger from security and data breaches. Access to the right tools that are up to date, operate effectively, and that keep you competitive and safe, is essential. On the other hand, having your head turned by the fanciest and most expensive software (even though it won't necessarily give you a competitive edge) undermines the work you've done on your budget!

Having access to the right computer and software, tools, and hardware is at least as important as a comfortable and functional space.

The amount of frustration that can be caused by slow or outdated IT, a constantly malfunctioning or inconveniently located printer, or tools not specific to the job in hand can go on to affect many other aspects of your team's work life. A stellar employee can become non-productive, slow, and grumpy if she is having to constantly battle to get her work done without the right equipment. I know I did. It matters. In whatever space we work in, we must also have the equipment we need to get our jobs done.

A step-by-step guide to assessing your environment

Getting your team to participate in this simple exercise can give you loads of valuable information in the analysis of your environment. Get everyone to note how the space affects them as they go about their day.

- As you approach your workspace, are you eager or dreading sitting down at your desk?
- Do you have the right equipment?
- Is there adequate adjustable lighting?
- Is the furniture in good condition and right for preventing bad backs and wrists?
- Can you adjust your space, especially if you have special requirements for vision impairment or a physical disability?
- Is there somewhere you can make drinks and store your lunch safely?
- Do you dread the minute you have to try and get the printer to work or download a large file?

- If you need to get people together to work on a project, is there the appropriate space and equipment for that?
- Can you invite clients in and feel like your environment supports your sale or credibility?

These are just some prompts to get people thinking. You can prompt with whatever questions you think are best for your situation.

You have more control over your environment than you think

You may think there is nothing you can do to change your environment, and there is probably little you can do structurally. But there is often more you can do that can have a real impact within your sphere of control than it may appear. Small things have the benefit of showing support for your staff and even compel your organisation to make some bigger changes by setting an example.

So, why did I move my team into a mouldy, dilapidated space with a wonky staircase?

We were spread across three sites, and every site was problematic. As is often the case in public sector organisations, our buildings were ancient and decrepit, hadn't been updated since the 1950s, and came with no budget for upkeep.

The bulk of my team were in a 1960's modern rabbit warren of a building, with each senior manager hived off in a closed-door office. When I first came on board, it seemed those managers never even left their offices.

I was based in another building across town from my team. It was a journey of only a few miles, but because of poor traffic design in the city, it could easily take 45 minutes or more (depending whether or not it was a market day). I was in a 1930's institution, isolated at the end of a remote corridor away from all of my fellow directors.

I recognised pretty early on that sorting out our accommodation had to be one of my top priorities. I also realised soon enough that it was not going to be easy.

I had a choice: leave us all hived away on opposite sides of town, in mediocre accommodation, letting team cohesion and collaboration continue to suffer, or bring us all together in dire accommodation. Now, as important as I believe accommodation is, I chose to bring us together.

The new (old) building was this mouldy, higgledy-piggledy structure with the irregular-sized rooms and poor configuration. It was stifling and noisy in summer and draughty in winter. The kitchen and bathrooms were ancient, and functionally poor.

After a struggle, I managed to get the buildings department to simply paint all the walls. It was basic, but it did go far in disguising the state of the walls and brightening the place up.

I then tasked my team with doing whatever they could to improve their space. The sky was the limit, as long as it didn't cost the organisation any money!

The process was a success. Being together in one space, albeit a terrible one, made an incredibly positive and immediate impact on our team cohesion. We got to know each other faster as we worked together to meet the challenges we were facing. We bonded over the improvement work. We laughed at the bizarre and inexplicable Heath Robinson-style solutions we uncovered from previous tenants as we constructed our own, which were even more laughable.

Now we had a united front against our unconventional and uncompromising space, and against the buildings team (who seemed determined to make even the smallest improvement an impossibility). We learned to joke about some of the more extreme quirks of our office space, and helped each other to tackle some of the worst ones. And we were simply all together in one place, with no one hiding down rabbit warren corridors.

What you can do to make a bad environment better

At first, I thought we were would be doomed to suffer in our workspace hell and often went home thinking *"What have I done?"*. But with a bit of ingenuity and determination, we managed to take our pig-of-a-space and dress it up with a little lipstick.

I hope you're not in a space that's worse than our mouldy, ramshackle building. But even if your space is simply not fit for purpose, there are ways to go about making it better. It is possible, with the help of your team, to create a more appropriate, productive environment.

When you have laid out your questions about the space and have gathered the answers from the exercise, you can decide how much time, energy, and resource to give to the issues that need a solution. Usually, you can quite easily determine if you have no, little, or total control over each one. Run through the list and code them red, yellow, or green, for instance, and then prioritise them.

For those you have total control over, these are no-brainers. Get a member of the team or someone with the right job in the organisation to get to work fixing them.

For those you have only a minor opportunity to impact, work with your team to think of work-arounds or alternative ways to tackle them that don't require full-on control. Some people are particularly good at this and rise to the challenge to come up with creative solutions.

It doesn't have to cost a lot of money. You can use modular storage and tabletops made from readily available materials (or even salvage materials), source cut price paint, and ask for volunteers to come in on a Saturday to spruce the place up. Most people would love to have the chance to make the space more enjoyable and comfortable since we all spend so much of our lives at work.

For those areas where you think you have no control, (or that are simply too expensive or insurmountable), there are two things you can do:

- First of all, be open and transparent with your team about why you won't be able to solve these issues. Again, people may be able to come up with a compromise or an alternative solution.
- But secondly, talk to your team about those that really do seem essential and that you agree are worth fighting upper management to change. It may be as simple as putting in a request or submitting a business case. Or it may be worth a full-on battle, an impassioned plea, or presenting some irrefutable evidence from individuals about how it impacts their work and getting things done.

If you have upper management or a leader who does not see the value in addressing the physical environment, especially if everything on the surface looks fine, it can be an uphill battle to get any improvement looked at. But trust me, your working environment is definitely something worth fighting for.

I fought for our new space, and in many ways it was still unsatisfactory after all of our hard work. It was just never going to be Buckingham Palace, or Google campus…

Still, I wouldn't have changed it for the world. What surprised me the most was how simply choosing to take action had positively affected the team. For years, their directors had done nothing. Previous leaders had chosen to make no decisions at all about the accommodation situation, good or bad. The fact that I at least acknowledged the problems and took decisive action to do something about it improved loyalty within the team, had a massive positive impact on our culture, and went on to help us get through a major threat to our very existence later.

The point here is not to give up, if for no other reason than to show your team just how important their comfort and ability to do their job is to you. This action will continue to build morale and team cohesion as people feel valued and listened to. You may be amazed at how creative you all become, too!

In summary

- The physical environment in which your team works has more influence over your productivity and morale than you may realise.
- Taking time to observe and ask questions before anything has gone too badly wrong can give you the chance to improve things for your team. This can also positively effect team culture.
- You have more control over your environment than you think. There are many things you can do within the confines of limited budgets or corporate restraints.
- Get your team involved; they may surprise you with their ingenuity to improve things.

- Simply taking action can have huge benefits in itself.

In the next chapter

Environment is one of the most practical and concrete elements of this model. It is, in some ways, both the easiest and most difficult to address and it's dangerous to underestimate its power. Get your team on board and you can do a lot in this area, much more than you may think is possible.

It is time now to look at all four parts of the model together and make a plan to get started and work through them. I have put the questions from each section into a workbook to make it as easy as possible for you to look at each one in turn with your team.

But before we move on to putting the model into practice, I want to share with you the top ten mistakes I have made over the years, so you don't have to:

What not to do (based on my own mistakes)

Fixing my 'lunchtime cliques' problem to improve our culture was surprisingly simple. I got lucky with that one; I got a lot of bang for my buck. I wasn't quite as fortunate with my physical environment problem- that was a complex situation with a less-than-ideal outcome. However, taking action turned out to be beneficial nonetheless. Regardless of outcome, the problems I've faced have all taught me something about what **not** to do:

1. Don't ignore problems hoping they'll go away.
2. Don't think because an issue is small it doesn't warrant any attention.
3. Don't think you know what is causing a problem with staffing, productivity, or effectiveness without actually investigating it and talking to people.
4. Don't think that just because nothing appears to be awry that all is fine. It may be. But unless you are getting out in your teams and talking to people and observing with your own eyes, you may miss an issue that could be nipped in the bud that would be twice as hard to deal with later.
5. Don't ever think a place runs itself. Get to know what is 'under the hood', and get some good systems and processes in place.
6. Don't ignore it when someone comes to you and tells you something is not right. Believe them until you have found out otherwise for yourself. Often people will not tell you directly using words- they will tell you through their actions. Learn to pick up the cues.
7. Don't think that just because people have access to the internet that they have the information they need and that this will make them effective and efficient.
8. Don't assume that you don't have any power over the physical environment in your workplace.
9. Don't think that culture is not a vitally important element of your team's success just because you can't see it.
10. And finally, don't try to fix anything alone!

Learn from past mistakes. (They don't have to be your own.) Each of these led me to develop a more in-depth understanding of the fundamental issues that had the biggest impact on the success of my teams. This four-part model will help you avoid these mistakes and address any issues faster and more effectively.

At this point, it is common for many people, especially experienced managers who may have led their teams for a while, to think that going through these elements with their team is a tedious and unnecessary process. I was thinking the same thing about my clique-ish staff problem. I thought it was petty and insubstantial. There is no telling what kind of staff relationship and productivity problems we could have ended up with if the resentments between staff had been left unchecked.

Keep going here, and you will see how this model can help you avoid all the mistakes on my well-worn list.

Chapter 8: How to put it all together and finish strong- The Workbook

In this book I have covered the most important fundamental areas that will help you overcome the struggles you may be having in your leadership or management role:

- Building a united team
- Conducting good, consistent, one-to-ones and performance reviews by implementing a simple system
- Using a four-part model to assess and troubleshoot the basic building blocks of your team

In this toolkit I bring it all together, providing you with simple, step-by-step guidance for becoming a fearless leader. It includes ready-to-use templates for the one-to-ones and performance reviews. For each of the four parts of the model, I provide you with questions to work through. I will give you an indication of how long you might want to spend on each, depending on how far you think your team is from where you want to be. I have also included some scales to score yourself on to help you determine that distance.

All teams can benefit from even a quick run through this model. You may have been leading your team for a while and know them and the business very well, or you may be a brand new manager with a new team and wondering how you are going to get a handle on the new job as quickly as possible. This toolkit will help you get a grip and improve things, no matter what your situation.

Finally, it is important not to treat this as a one-off exercise. Revisit it at least once a year to make sure things haven't drifted or regressed. Old habits die hard.

A little regular tune-up can make all the difference to your team's performance.

Whether you choose to go through the workbook systematically or not, you should have gained a level of awareness of the important elements of managing and leading a team that will be valuable to you in your role. Congratulations on being one of the good ones; on being a leader who wants to do better by their team.

You can get full-size pdfs of all the materials that follow, get further information, and see the services that I offer on my website at www.elizabethshassere.com.

You can contact me at: elizabeth@elizabethshassere.com or on twitter @startupliz. I would love to hear about your experiences of using the tools in this book and applying the lessons learned.

I wish you and your teams well.

One-to-one and performance review forms

This is the one-to-one form I use for my teams:

Employee Name **Date**
1. Informal discussion 2. Current workload and priorities update 3. Update on progress against objectives 4. Key issues/action forward
Current workload and priorities update (to be completed by the team member prior to the meeting)
Update on progress against objectives (to be completed by the team member prior to the meeting)
Key issues/action forward (for the manager to complete based on the discussion and shared with the team member)

This is the performance review form I use for my teams:

Employee Name
Date

1. Informal discussion
2. Review of progress against objectives
3. Notes on achievement of objectives
4. Workload review
5. Professional development needs
6. Key issues/action forward

Review of progress against objectives (to be completed by the team member prior to the meeting)

Notes on achievement of objectives (to be completed by the manager)

Workload review (to be completed by the manager)

Professional development needs (to be completed by team member prior to the meeting)

Key issues/action forward (for the manager to complete based on the discussion and shared with the team member)

Taking your team through the model: guidance and questions for each section

How far are you from where you want to be?

As you read through the previous chapters, you will have recognised some issues present in your own team. Some things may have really struck a nerve, and you instantly felt a pang of recognition in your gut that your team needs help. You may also have felt pretty smug about other areas, maybe not only feeling like you and your team are doing well in them, but you may even have ideas that go far beyond what is covered here.

Most teams will have some areas that need a lot of work and some areas that need virtually no attention at all, and of course, many areas in between.

Before you get started, it is worth taking some time to think about what your starting point is.

First, I will pose several questions that might help you get an honest picture of where you are.

Then, I will give you a sliding scale for each area to help you prioritise what you might focus on.

Some questions to get you started:

1. Is this your first management position or first time leading a team?
2. How long have you been managing your current team?
3. Do you have a new boss?

4. How well do you feel your team is doing right now? Are they working well together? Is their performance high?
5. Do you believe there are elements of your team, their work, or their environment that could be improved?

Take five minutes here to make a list of the five top things that most need improvement in your team. (Do this before you go through the rest of the model.) Don't think too hard about it, just write the first five things that come to mind.

Take another five minutes to think about the best aspects of your team. What's working well? What are the strengths of your team? Again, don't ponder too long, just write what immediately comes to mind.

Now let's drill down a bit into what you have written. Take twenty minutes to expand on each point. How do you really feel about your work and your team?

1. How often do you feel overwhelmed or as though you don't know what you're doing? Do you worry you will be found out not to have an adequate grip on things?
2. How do you feel on a Sunday night thinking about Monday morning at work?
3. Do you feel proud of the work you do as a manager, or do you feel like you are letting your team down?
4. What areas of improvement would take your team from ok to excellent?

5. What has your boss mentioned to you in recent months that he or she would like you to improve upon in your area of responsibility?

6. In what areas is performance poorer than you would like? Where would you like your team to shine?

7. Where have you noticed team performance, team relationships, or output and productivity starting to slide?

8. What areas would benefit if your team had greater focus? Are you struggling with focusing everyone on the same goals? What are the competing priorities or where is there territoriality amongst team members?

9. How are you managing to keep up with your work leading the team? Are you struggling to pin down the causes of some of the problems you see?

10. If you had a better relationship with your team, what things would be easier or more enjoyable about your job?

Feeling proud of what you do and confident in how you do it is the key to being an excellent leader with a good team following. Going through this toolkit will help you get there.

A simple score sheet for taking stock

Now that you have thought through the questions above, take five more minutes and place you and your team where you think you are on the spectrum for each part. (You can get a full-size pdf of this scoresheet from my website at www.elizabethshassere.com)

Do this quickly:

Building a united team

1	2	3	4	5	6	7	8	9	10

My team feels like a bunch of individuals that just come in every day, do their jobs, and go home.

My team are loyal and committed to each other and our work. We treat each other with respect, and support each other to achieve our goals.

One-to-ones and performance reviews

1	2	3	4	5	6	7	8	9	10

I don't meet regularly with people who report directly to me to keep up with how they are doing. They don't have a system for the people they manage either, or I don't know if they do.

We have a system of one-to-ones and performance management. They are scheduled in and happen regularly. They are documented and this documentation is shared between the manager and the staff member.

Mission statement, values, and goals

1	2	3	4	5	6	7	8	9	10

We don't have a written mission statement. We don't discuss values or have any agreed as a team. We don't have goals that are written down.

We have developed and written a mission statement that is up to date and relevant. Values are an important part of how we have created a culture that represents who we are as a team. We have shared goals that are written down that all of our work is aligned to.

Culture

1	2	3	4	5	6	7	8	9	10

I don't understand the concept of culture and what it means for my team. I don't see the importance of this.

As a leader, I have worked hard with my team to create a culture that we all want to work in, that reflects our mission statement and values, and that attracts some of the best talent in the industry.

Knowledge and information

1	2	3	4	5	6	7	8	9	10

People just muddle on and deal with their own information needs. There isn't a system for this. We are lacking some key skills in our team (or they are not applied effectively and efficiently).

We have a way of dealing with information which means we have got this Goldilocks element just right. Staff have ready access to what they need without being overwhelmed and wasting time. We have a good skill mix that supports our business and we prioritise developing staff skills and invest in their future in the team.

Environment

1	2	3	4	5	6	7	8	9	10

Our workspace is not fit for purpose. Either the size or functionality isn't appropriate or it is uncomfortable or unattractive. It affects our productivity It makes it hard for us to recruit.

We have taken the time and put in the effort to make our workspace fit for purpose, comfortable, and attractive. Even if we didn't have a budget for this, we have come together as a team to improve what we could. Our space is a big draw in our recruitment. We are proud to bring customers and clients here.

How do your scales look? Are there a few areas that are worryingly low? Does everything look depressingly average, and maybe you would like to strive for excellence in some areas? No problem. Going through the sets of questions in the four parts of the model will help you improve things no matter where you are starting.

The point of this exercise was first of all to help you prioritise, then to help you begin to think about how much time and resource you might want to put into each one.

- For those areas you scored at **three or below**, you may need a big change in how you do things. I would suggest these areas need significant time and a commitment to resources to improve. You may want to think about bringing in external facilitators, or consultants, to help do this work. This would keep your team focused on their jobs and not take their time away from the business. An investment in these areas could pay out many times over, by solving debilitating problems for your team. Also, depending on how sensitive or contentious the areas are, having an objective outsider take you through it could save a lot of friction in the team.
- For areas **between 4 and 6**, think about how they are affecting the team's work and morale or your ability to be competitive in your industry. They may need an intensive, whole-team approach. You may need to carve time out of the day job for you and your team to focus on this work. It may be worth more than a bit of lost productivity now to make a full-scale improvement on areas that will boost

productivity for years to come. Working through the questions in the model will help you target your efforts and strike a balance between investment for improvement and return on that investment.

- For those areas you **scored a 7 to 10,** congratulations and well done on having some strong, well-performing aspects of your team! However, it's important not to get complacent in these areas. They will not be highly-performing by accident. Your team will be giving these areas due time and attention to achieve this. They may only require an annual evaluation and a bit of tweaking, but if left neglected, they may start to slide and cause you problems later. Simply giving them some cursory attention can help keep these areas healthy and performing well. It will also be worth having a look at why those areas are doing so well and seeing if you can share any good practices to improve other areas.

Getting your team on board

Bringing your team along with you on this journey is important. Nothing sabotages progress more than imposing programmes of work or big changes on a team without their engagement up front.

At the same time, only you will know what the state of your current relationship is with your team. If things are too contentious, or if you are brand new to the team, full engagement may be something that has to be built up over time. Some of the problems you have identified may not be able to wait for that.

The most important thing is to be as open and transparent as possible in all the work that you do as a leader. You can quickly get people on side when they realise you are committed to making improvements.

Take a bit of a temperature check with your team:

1. How long have you been working together?
2. Do you have regular face-to-face meetings and see each other in the office most days?
3. Is the culture open and friendly, with wide-ranging conversations about personal lives as well as work?
4. Do you have a relaxed, personable atmosphere, or a formal, conservative one?

Matching the tone of the existing culture will make introducing this work much more palatable.

Bear in mind there are always people who are afraid of change or who feel that the current situation hides a multitude of sins, perhaps theirs, such as low productivity or poor skills. They may think it's in their interest to hinder any efforts on your part to analyse the state of things and make improvements. Engage them up front, and involve them in the process early. Otherwise, you may find yourself with people sabotaging your progress with this work.

What follows now are each of the four parts of the model with a full set of questions to help you get the answers you need to make real improvements for your team.

How to fix the problems you find

One of the benefits of this model is that often, just by going through the guided thinking provided by the description of each part and the sets of questions, you will immediately see solutions and ways to improve the things you recognise. Some problems that seemed complex and difficult before can become simple and with obvious answers. Most teams will benefit just from talking about the issues. Sometimes shining a light on certain things, or sharing concerns and realising that many of your teammates share the same problems, can go a long way to bringing the change that is needed.

Of course, some problems will not be so easy! These problems will need a plan that has to be implemented over time. For instance, things like gaps in knowledge require developing job descriptions and recruitment processes; problems with IT may need research into the best software solutions and their procurement. Changes to the environment may mean a schedule of works and disruption to the workspace. If you have identified what needs to happen, it should be more than worth the hassle for the improvement it will bring.

One final but very important point: It is vital that you, as a leader, take action once you have worked through these questions with your team. If you don't, you risk losing their trust and their confidence in you as a manager. (Especially if the team has put in extra time to support the efforts, abandoning action and solutions will bring hard feelings and resentment.) So, get ready to commit to doing it, or being honest and transparent when you can't.

Develop your mission statement, values, and goals to motivate and inspire

Questions to guide your thinking

1. What is our overall mission?
2. What do we come in to do every day?
3. What are we striving for? What do we want to achieve the most?
4. How do we fit into the bigger picture (if we are part of a larger organisation)?
5. What is our ideal vision for the life of the company?
6. What does the work that our organisation does stand for?
7. Where do we want to be as a team in 5 years?
8. What do we want our legacy to be?
9. Do all team members know our mission, values, and goals?
10. What would make us feel proud to have achieved as a team?

Assess your culture and make it what you want

The questions to determine your culture and any underlying issues with it

Internal questions for the team

1. What does it feel like to work here? Exciting? Comfortable? Boring?
2. What does it feel like to be a part of this team?
3. What is appealing about working here?
4. Is there an overt hierarchy in our department?
5. Is this a useful or destructive hierarchy?
6. Do people feel valued and respected?
7. Do people socialise together, either during the workday for example at lunchtime, or after work?
8. What are the things you dread the most when you think about coming to work each day?
9. What part of working here do you enjoy the most?
10. Is there anything you miss about your job when you are away on leave for a week or two, or even for the weekend?
11. What one thing, if changed, would make the biggest difference to your work life?
12. Have you considered leaving due to some part of the workplace atmosphere that affects you negatively? If so, what was that thing?
13. What is the best thing about working here?
14. What is the worst thing about working here?
15. If someone asks you at a dinner party, what would you say about your workplace?

As the leader, ask yourself

1. Do people care about the work that is being done, or do they just do the work for a pay cheque?
2. Do you have one or two "problematic" team members who are contentious, or who are generally unpleasant to be around, or worse, destructive and undermining?
3. Do you praise staff and acknowledge when there is a job well done?
4. Do your staff go the extra mile for you either when asked or voluntarily?
5. Do you often ask them to?
6. What modes of encouragement do you use?
7. Do you show appreciation when staff do something for you, especially if it is above and beyond their normal job role such as when they have to turn something around quickly, work late, or drop what they are working on to help you?

From the outside looking in:

1. If you are part of a larger department or organisation, what is that culture like?
2. How are we perceived by the outside world- both the rest of the organisation and external to it?
3. What kinds of clients/customers does our image appeal to?
4. What does our publicity or advertising say about us? How is it perceived by the outside world?
5. What is the overall impression that our company gives?
6. Do lots of people strive to work here, or do we struggle to fill positions?

Get your knowledge and information just right

Knowledge

Start this section with your function and skills mapping as described in Chapter 6: Knowledge and Information.

What functions do we perform every day? Monthly, quarterly, yearly? All functions count. If you don't rely on them to keep the wheels turning, question why you keep doing them. Don't forget the functions within your workspace, for instance, are the bins being emptied and are office supplies being ordered?

Once you have laid out the functions, consider:

1. What skills does each function require?
2. Do we have the right skill set within our organisation to fulfil each function?
3. What specialist and generic skills are needed? What ones are we missing in our team?
4. Which functions are outsourced or bought in? Is internal or external more effective and efficient?
5. Would some functions be cheaper to buy in as and when we need it, and not take on the cost of employment of a permanent individual? Or should we build up the necessary skill in-house?
6. Do we support people to develop their technical and professional skills within their work day?
7. What hidden transferable skills might people have from a previous role or perhaps even volunteering? What things do people really enjoy doing, which may not currently be part of their existing role?

8. Are there areas of their job people are lacking confidence in, or lacking the necessary support to do well? Where do they think additional training or learning would help them go from "getting by" to excelling?

9. With the addition of a certain skill, could we improve efficiency or performance, or reduce staff costs in another area? Can some individuals safely fulfil multiple needs?

Information

Start this section with your function and skills mapping that you did as part of the Knowledge and information section

Get each individual to list the data and information that is essential for them to do their job.

1. Do we have the information we need to do our jobs well?
2. Is it easy to access and to use?
3. What would be "nice to have" or what would give us a competitive advantage?
4. What is our biggest complaint in relation to data and information? What are our biggest frustrations?

Financial information

1. What do we spend the bulk of our budget on?
2. Which part of our work brings in the most money?
3. What is the one category of spend that pays off the most in bringing in business and income?

4. What area of spending appears to be neglected as far as investment is concerned?
5. What category jumps out at us as being most wasteful?
6. What one thing could we spend more on that would have a positive impact on our income or the service we provide?
7. What one thing could we cut out altogether that would have little or no impact on our work?

Improve your environment for a big impact

1. Is this a comfortable and functional place to work?
2. How does it feel when we walk in the door every morning?
3. Is it the appropriate size and functionality?
4. Does it promote productivity, morale, and efficiency?
5. What would make it better?
6. Is the location good for staff to feel integral to the surrounding community or is it isolated? Can people go out at lunchtime or during breaks quickly enough to fit errands or exercise into their day?
7. Is the location convenient, giving employees a choice in how to travel there?
8. What does the location say to our clients?
9. Does the standard of accommodation suit our industry?
10. Is the cost putting a strain on our finances?

Exercise for all team members to complete

1. As you approach your workspace, are you eager or dreading sitting down at your desk?
2. Do you have the right equipment at hand?
3. Is there adequate adjustable lighting?
4. Is the furniture in good condition and right for preventing bad backs and wrists?
5. Can you adjust your space, especially if you have special requirements for vision impairment or a physical disability?
6. Is there somewhere you can make drinks and store your lunch safely?

7. Do you dread the minute you have to try and get the printer to work, or download a large file?
8. If you need to get people together to work on a project, is there space and equipment for that?
9. Can you invite clients in and feel like your environment supports your sales or credibility?

Conclusion: Discovering your managerial superpowers

Remember, it's important not to treat this exercise as a one-off, but to keep in mind what it has shown you as you progress through the year. I would recommend going through the model's questions as a quick, desktop exercise at least yearly. This lets you see if things have drifted or regressed into old habits that could make performance or morale start to slide. If you have had new team members come on board, or have lost some, it is a good idea to take that into consideration when timing a review.

A regular tune-up can make a big difference to performance with very little time and effort once you have done the initial analysis. You now know as much as you can about your team and things that affect their work the most.

I think it is worth repeating here my list of top ten lessons of what not to do as a manager, ever:

1. Don't ignore problems hoping they'll go away.
2. Don't think because an issue is small it doesn't warrant any attention.
3. Don't think you know what is causing a problem with staffing, productivity, or effectiveness without actually investigating it and talking to people.
4. Don't think that just because nothing appears to be awry that all is fine. It may be, but unless you are getting out in your teams and talking to people and observing with your own eyes, you may miss an

issue that could be nipped in the bud that would be twice as hard to deal with later.

5. Don't ever think a place runs itself. Get to know what is "under the hood", and get some good systems and processes in place.

6. Don't ignore it when someone comes to you and tells you something is not right. Believe them until you have found out otherwise for yourself. Often people will not tell you directly in words- they will tell you through their actions. Learn to pick up the cues.

7. Don't think that just because people have access to the internet they have the information they need and that this will make them effective and efficient.

8. Don't assume that you don't have any power over the physical environment in your workplace.

9. Don't think that culture is not a vitally important element of your team's success just because you can't see it.

10. And finally, don't try to fix anything alone!

So, what did you learn about yourself as a manager? Having been through this work with your team, you may have found out that you get a lot out of managing a team through challenges and change. Maybe it brought you closer together and has improved your relationship with them. It may have boosted your confidence and the feeling of being in control of your work. You may simply realise you are good at managing and leading teams. You can harness the power of what you have just gone through to be better than ever, and you can always revisit the model to give you a boost when you are feeling overwhelmed or if things with your team are starting to slide.

Good luck with managing your team, and becoming an even better leader. And congratulations on being one of the good ones who wants to do better, be better, and become fearless.

List of workbook materials

One-to-one and performance review forms

- One-to-one form
- Performance review form

How far are you from where you want to be?

- Some questions to get you started
- Top five things that need improvement
- The strengths of your team
- Drilling down into what matters most

A simple score sheet for taking stock

- Score sheet

Getting your team on board

- Take a temperature check

Mission statement, values, and goals

- Questions to guide your thinking

Culture

- Internal questions for your team
- Questions for the leader
- From the outside looking in

Knowledge and information

- Considering staff skills and capacity
- Analysing information needs
- Thinking strategically about finances

Environment

- Questions about your workplace environment
- Environment exercise for all team members

Index of hyperlinks referenced in the text

Imposter Syndrome:
https://en.wikipedia.org/wiki/Impostor_syndrome or
search for "imposter syndrome" or "feeling like a
fraud"

The Peter Principle:
https://en.wikipedia.org/wiki/Peter_principle or
search for "The Peter Principle" or "Laurence J. Peter"

Personal development model:
https://www.hoffmaninstitute.org/ or search for
"Hoffman Process"

Team collaboration tools:
http://uk.pcmag.com/software/70214/guide/the-best-online-collaboration-software-of-2017 or search for
"best team collaboration tools"

Mission Statements:

Google: https://www.google.co.uk/about/our-company/ or search for "Google mission statement"

Patagonia: http://www.patagonia.com/company-info.html or search for "Patagonia mission statement"

Amazon: https://www.amazon.jobs/working/working-amazon or go to Amazon's Facebook page.

Kaiser Permanente:
https://share.kaiserpermanente.org/about-kaiser-

permanente/ or search for "Kaiser Permanente mission statement"

Website of mission statements: https://www.missionstatements.com/company_missio n_statements.html or search for "best mission statements" or "most inspirational mission statements"

Textocracy: https://textocracy.org/ or search for "Textocracy"

Zappos core values: https://www.zappos.com/core-values or search for "Zappos core values"

About the Author

Weekly blog on Medium.com: https://medium.com/@eshassere or search for "Medium Elizabeth Shassere"

Learn more about how you can participate in a Startup Weekend and why you should: https://startupweekend.org/ or search for "techstars startup weekend"

Quotes

"…in every organization everyone rises to the level at which they become paralyzed with fear." -Seth Godin, Tribes (2008)

"I always tell people that fearlessness is not the absence of fear, it's the mastery of fear. Fearlessness is about getting up one more time than we fall down — or are tripped by our critics!" -Ariana Huffington, From: *A Conversation Between Arianna and Her Daughters*, THE BLOG, 04/09/2007 11:36 am ET **Updated** Nov 17, 2011 on huffingtonpost.com.

"In winning companies, everybody pulls in the same direction". -Steve Blank, From: *Watching Larry Ellison become Larry Ellison — The DNA of a Winner*, posted on September 25, 2014 by steveblank on steveblank.com.

"Just being available and attentive is a great way to use listening as a management tool. Some employees will come in, talk for twenty minutes, and leave having solved their problems entirely by themselves." - Nicholas V. Luppa, search for "Nicholas V. Luppa" and "listening"

"Everything should be made as simple as possible, but no simpler." -Albert Einstein (See the attribution of this derivation at https://quoteinvestigator.com/2011/05/13/einstein-simple/)

"Mission statements […] have a purpose. The purpose [is] to force management to make hard decisions about what the company [stands] for. A hard decision means giving up one thing to get another." -Seth Godin, From: *Not even close--the worst mission statements...*, posted on January 25, 2005 by Seth Godin, sethgodin.typepad.com.

"A **vision statement** is a vivid idealized description of a desired outcome that inspires, energizes and helps you create a mental picture of your target. It could be a vision of a part of your life, or the outcome of a project or goal. ... vision statements are often confused with mission statements, but they serve complementary purposes.", From: *Writing a Compelling Vision Statement,* http://www.timethoughts.com/goalsetting/vision-statements.htm

"It turns out that what actually separates thriving organizations from struggling ones are the difficult-to-measure attitudes, processes and perceptions of the people who do the work. Culture defeats strategy, every time." *–Seth Godin*, From: *Let's stop calling them 'soft skills'*, posted on January 31, 2017 by Seth Godin, itsyourturnblog.com

"We are drowning in information but starved for knowledge." -John Naisbitt, search for "John Naisbitt" and "information"

"[The building you work in] is a culture and values issue worth fighting over." -Steve Blank, From: *The Curse of a New Building,* posted on May 15, 2009 by steveblank on steveblank.com

Acknowledgements

Thank you to beta readers and moral supporters for giving me your time, encouragement, and practical help: Baiju Shah, Laura IH Bennett, Samantha Deakin-Hill, Ingrid Ablett-Spence, Mihaela Gruia, Giorgio Cassella, Jamie Veitch, Darren Chouings, Ann Shassere, Jeanne Dunn, Kisha Bradley, and Catherine Huby. Thank you to my editor Parul MacDonald for her invaluable guidance and instruction through this, my first book. And to my editor Ellen Holcombe, who is truly a professional Word Person. A special thank you to co-workers and staff at the University of Sheffield Enterprise for support, patience, and being willing to teach me so many new and valuable skills that allowed me to get this book finished. Last but certainly not least, thank you to the people who have been part of my teams over the years who taught me some of the best lessons I could have asked for as a leader.

About the Author

Elizabeth Shassere built, led, and managed teams of all sizes throughout her twenty-year career in health services and local government. Elizabeth successfully took these teams through programmes of transformation and improvement during times of significant policy and political change. She has studied and worked in the United States and the United Kingdom, and has experience from the local to the national level in both countries.

Elizabeth recently left her public sector career to start her own company. Textocracy provides an accessible feedback and public consultation data collection service that provides data for improving products and services that better meet users' needs. She provides expertise on digital transformation, and advocates for digital transformation for inclusion.

Elizabeth shares her lessons learned in leadership and management through coaching and mentoring, and on her weekly Medium blog. She also gives back to the community that helped her become a tech startup founder and entrepreneur with no previous experience by volunteering at Startup Weekends and speaking at various forums.

You can contact Elizabeth at:
elizabeth@elizabethshassere.com or on twitter @startupliz.

For materials related to this book, further information, and to see the services she offers go to
www.elizabethshassere.com.

Made in the USA
Middletown, DE
09 March 2019